O UGHTEN
H OUSE
PUBLICATIONS

"Ascension Books for the Rising Planetary Consciousness"

DEDICATION

I dedicate this work to the bearers of Light and Love the world over, in whatever guise you find yourselves cloaked — to those past, present, and yet unborn, who render genuine service from the heart on behalf of harmony and understanding, within and among all peoples.

Intuition by Design

by Victor R. Beasley, Ph.D.

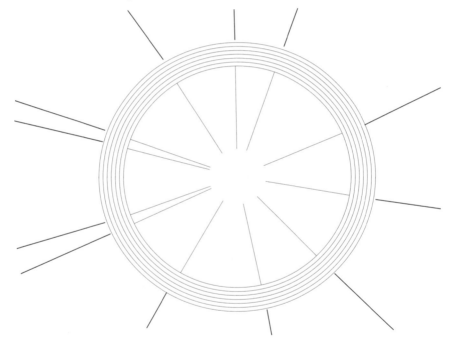

Applying Your Intuitive Intelligence
for Personal and Business Decision-Making

(Introducing The IQ Geometrics)

INTUITION BY DESIGN
Applying Your Intuitive Intelligence
for Personal and Business Decision-Making

© 1992, 1995 by Victor R. Beasley
Published 1993. Second Edition 1995.

00 99 98 97 96 95   0 9 8 7 6 5 4 3 2 1

Second Edition

EDITING & TYPOGRAPHY BY SARA BENJAMIN-RHODES

Published by:
OUGHTEN HOUSE PUBLICATIONS
P.O. Box 2008
Livermore, California, 94551-2008 USA

Library of Congress Cataloging-in-Publication Data
Beasley, Victor R., 1939-
    Intuition by design : applying your intuitive intelligence for personal and business decision-making / by Victor R. Beasley
            p.   cm.
        ISBN 1-880666-22-7 : $21.95
        1. Intuition (Psychology).   2. Decision-making. 3. Self-help.
    I. Title.
    HD38.B356   1994
    658.4'03--dc20   94-18042
                                                CIP
ISBN 1-880666-22-7, Trade Publication
            Printed in United States of America
        Printed with vegetable ink on acid-free paper

CONTENTS

ACKNOWLEDGMENTS

What, truly, does one ever do on one's own? Is it even possible for a person to achieve *anything* without the aid of some divine agency — something which extends beyond the familiar boundaries which we know as our personality, our training, our conscious-mind, or our mundane experience? Consider that Universal Intelligence is the animating and sustaining force behind our every achievement: it exists in the very breath that we breathe for life itself; in the friend who offers words of encouragement just when you need it; in the brilliant idea that pops into your head "out of nowhere," just when you are feeling blocked creatively. Consider that in your parents, in your elementary school teacher, and in every human being that you ever encountered — for better or worse — that was God supporting you in moving from one achievement to the next.

So it is with this present work. Here, I can but mention some of those heaven-sent entities whose immediate contributions have made this volume possible. First, I acknowledge a loving, guiding presence — a flow of Divine Grace, which regularly and gently enfolds my linear-thinking mind within a broader sphere of intuitive knowing. This divine support makes possible insights, inspiration, and impressions that are otherwise not available to me.

My wife, Michelle Grace, has been a constant and sustaining source of light in moving through the many phases of this project — proofing, editing, re-proofing, advising, encouraging ... whatever it took. This volume was given birth because she nurtured it along. From the beginning, Aida Ferrarone (my dear friend of many years) was ever-present with validation and support for the IQ Cards. And in the initial stages, Lita Charlot generously volunteered to do the typesetting of the Cards' verse.

With much patience and professionalism, Julie Wellen retyped each successive version of the manuscript. Jan Becker and Mary Westheimer gave insightful suggestions and, here in Phoenix, our Intuition Network Group tested the IQ Cards in their personal and business affairs and provided important feedback.

My thanks go to Ed Azoyan for his exacting AutoCad expertise in drawing the IQ Geometrics. This saved me countless hours of creating each Geometric by hand. My appreciation, too, to my business colleagues at *Resource:* Bob Roberts, Roy Geer, Julie Rosskopf, Jack Root, and Elizabeth Becker, who each in her/his own way gave suggestions and support during the formative stages of this work. Elizabeth's help in the computer formatting of the IQ Geometrics was invaluable.

My friend, Arnold Patent, enthusiastically encouraged me to move ahead with this work at a time when I was still wondering if the expansion of intuition via geometric wavefields made sense to anyone except myself.

Meeting again with my spiritual brother, Sri Sant Keshavadas, twenty years after our first meeting in Guyana, South America, brings a timely blessing to this work. His unfailing encouragement to expand the reach of this volume to include many countries is especially gratifying.

There was an instantaneous affinity with Robert Gerard and his staff at Oughten House, with *Intuition By Design* ... a very confirming experience, indeed. Sara Benjamin's outstanding editorial skills lift this edition to a new level of excellence.

To those who, in any way, supported the production of this volume, my loving thanks to you all.

INTRODUCTION

— Blessings —

Intuition By Design is a very appealing and practical book. It is especially useful for learning to apply one's intuition toward achieving constructive personal decision-making and successful business enterprises.

Since time immemorial, the sages of the Himalayas have known that there is only one faculty in man — called intuition — through which he can realize the Truth. It is nothing but the Light of consciousness. This faculty could be developed through divine knowledge, devotional love, selfless service, or through meditation. Until now, this faculty was used for knowing the higher spheres, angels, and archangels, and for spiritual enlightenment.

Now for the first time, integrating geometric principles known to ancient Rishis in the East, Dr. Beasley has made using the intuitive intelligence for a successful career or business a possibility. He has outlined seven aspects of intuitive decision-making, and has clearly discussed intuitive methods. This is useful, for it makes it more feasible for one to live day-to-day according to the teachings of eternal wisdom.

Being deeply religious — in the spiritual, universal sense of the word — Dr. Beasley has combined the thoughts of the East and the West. This could be very inspiring for young businessmen and women, the world over, who seek such a synthesis in their own lives.

I wish him success in his endeavor, and I am positive that he will write many more books as guidelines for people, especially the younger generation. May God bless him and all the readers of this book, and users of the IQ Cards, to develop intuition and peace.

OM and Prem,
Sant Keshavadas

Truth is One, many are the Names

PREFACE

"A man should learn to detect and watch for that gleam of light which flashes across his mind from within, more than the luster of the firmament of bards and sages."

Ralph Waldo Emerson

CAUTION! This volume and accompanying IQ (Intuition Quotient) Cards constitute a consciousness alignment instrument, the function of which is to refine the balance between *The Wisdom of The Heart* and *The Action of The Mind.* Your life may be permanently altered by its use, for such is the way of true intuition. It has been said that true intuition is the movement of Spirit within one's heart. This was true for the ancient Egyptians — particularly during Akhnaton's 18th Dynasty — for whom *Intelligence of The Heart* meant: "intuition and intellect bonded in a blissful marriage within one's own consciousness."

Why do we look outside of ourselves for answers that we already carry within? Why do we force solutions that don't fit and, against our own better judgment, willingly endure that which is toxic to body, mind, and spirit? What, at last, do we gain by ignoring the gentle precision of our "still small voice" within, in favor of the harsh dominance of the rational mind?

As homo sapiens, we are innately endowed with the faculty of creative insight through spontaneous, intuitive knowing. Intuition and intellect are intended as partners, not adversaries competing in a win/lose fight to the death. Intuitive potential is part of our birthright as a species. There is no need for us to remain blinded to Spirit's reality, or to be held in bondage by linear thinking and historical precedent. *Intuitive intelligence* is the key to liberating ourselves from the dark ages of personal self-doubt, past fears, social prejudice, and global mistrust.

This work introduces the use of ancient geometric technology which has been updated for contemporary use. Geometric technology, for consciousness enhancement does not rely upon the historical authority of a particular culture — it is confirmed by all cultures. The eternal principles of geometric forcefields are operative in the arts, architecture, and rituals of peoples the world over. Geometric wavefields have about them a self-validating authenticity, which appeals directly to one's awakening intuitive sense-perception. The universality of this geometric wisdom-tradition constitutes a kind of ecumenical bonding between divergent cultural traditions: a Cosmic Truth embracing the many into a powerful, unanimous statement of *Oneness,* a single unifying reality transcending the limitations and prejudices of any single culture. Divine geometry pre-dates history and provides a means through which Spirit ensouls civilizations.

The accompanying IQ Cards consist of thirty-six cards which are subdivided into three categories of twelve cards each. The cards carry a geometric pattern on one side and verse on the other. The function of each card is to guide the individual to his clearest possible intuitive knowing concerning a significant, compelling issue currently affecting his life. In effect, the IQ Cards are a bridge, linking intuition and intellect, joining together in harmonious tandem that part of you that "knows" with that part of you which makes the decisions.

Additionally — like the notes of the musical scale, the letters of the alphabet, or the primary colors — the thirty-six IQ Cards can be used in numerous combinations and sequences to create etheric environments that are tailored to, and expressive of, the needs of the individual or the group. In effect, the IQ Cards provide you with a technology for loving your Self ... a practical means of honoring and valuing — above all else — that aspect of your consciousness that is One with *Universal Intelligence.*

The purpose, then, of this volume and the accompanying IQ Cards is to support the unfolding of the fullest potential of each one who uses them. This purpose is essentially threefold:

1. To promote for the individual a clearer *intuitive sense-perception* founded upon love and eternal universal principles ... an expanded view of reality with which to approach day-to-day decision-making.

2. To establish functional frameworks for taking *purposeful action* (Soul-directed action) towards resolving situations, challenges, and problems which arise in business, daily living, personal growth, and inter-ethnic communications.

3. To help each of us to truly comprehend the events of our lives as neither "good" nor "bad", but rather as instructive, corrective feedback for maintaining clear, undistorted alignment between our inner knowing and our outer actions.

It is my intention that this work be for you an instrument of Light, serving the *intelligence of your heart*. Yet I realize that this present approach to intuitive decision-making may not be suited to everyone. Indeed, many valid paths lead to intuitive awareness. But for those who do resonate to the frequencies of the IQ Cards, I wish you a joyful journey via their verse and geometrics. Truly, it is by design that we are beings of both intuition and intellect. And this volume is an invitation to experience that highest union of feeling and thinking — *The Intelligence of The Heart* — in all of your affairs.

Victor R. Beasley
Phoenix, Arizona
April 11, 1994

"God geometrizes."
Dr. Albert Einstein

GOD GEOMETRIZES

The Physicist Priest

It had been a beautiful Indian Summer's day in Cheltenham, England. The vast green lawns of the Commons were bordered by a profusion of bright flowers and manicured gardens, which proliferated throughout this timeless village. It was an idyllic masterpiece, a visual feast that Van Gogh himself would have relished.

The conference ended. And now, the early dark of an October evening advanced quickly. William Scott, a local businessman who enjoyed dabbling in alternative healing, had invited several of us over to his place for tea, where we could continue the conference themes. Congenial good-byes were shared all around and within minutes I found myself speeding along the winding roads of an English countryside at dusk, ensconced in a sedan full of newly acquired friends. Among them was a jocular Catholic Priest by the name of Father Andrew Glazewski. He had impishly informed us that the best way to remember the pronunciation of his name was to think "glass-o-whisky."

Shortly afterward, we arrived at William's home. It was straight out of an English novel or historical movie. We entered this large stone cottage, originally built somewhere around the 15th century — rustic, weathered, ancient, enduring the passage of time. The structure featured low door beams designed for medieval five-footers. Obviously, those diminutive architects of the era of King Richard III had not anticipated my 20th Century visit in a 6'4" body — a clear example of short-sighted planning!

There were about eight of us all settled in around the cozy hearth as the priest began to speak. "Who would like to volunteer for a demonstration?" he asked. Father Andrew was revered and widely known in England. Not only was he a clergyman ... he was also distinguished as a physicist and as a phenomenal natural healer. All this, to my mind, was a most unlikely and illogical combination of talents. How could anyone — much less a priest — be both a scientist and healer? In my world, these two disciplines scarcely acknowledged each other, and now here they were combined within a single human mind! This did not compute. "Surely this poor fellow must be schizoid," I reasoned quietly. "I will! You can work on me," volunteered a man two spaces to my left.

Father Andrew moved into position in front of the man, who was still sitting near me. As I watched, Father

Andrew's sensitive hands deftly sliced the air around the man's body with the grace and precision of a Balinese dancer. There was no physical contact. He simply moved his hands — first one, then the other, then both — back and forth and around the man's torso in what looked to me like a regular path or pattern. "There!" he suddenly announced, after about a minute and a half of silent examination. "This is where the problem is." The priest's right hand was nearly two feet away from his subject's body. How could the chronic intestinal discomfort of which the man had earlier complained have its origins out there in mid-air? I thought, "Perhaps all this guy really needs is a good laxative." "It's right here," Glazewski insisted. "Come put your hand here," he encouraged as he guided my hand to occupy the space where his own had been. "Hmm," I grunted cautiously, "I'm not sure I feel anything." "Of course," he persisted. "You can even see the lines." With this revelation, things were definitely starting to move way beyond my familiar three-dimensional comfort zone. Nothing in my academic background or life experience had prepared me for this. Though I looked where he was looking, I saw no energy lines.

I was beginning to question Father Andrew's sanity. Here was a "man of the cloth," a respected scientist and spiritual authority, feeling and seeing lines of energy about which my physical senses had no clue. It was most disconcerting. The others of our party just sat looking astonished. I began to wonder if I would have to convert to Catholicism or take a vow of celibacy in order to master these exotic healing techniques!

The demonstration continued with Father Andrew's explanation of the various energy bodies which parallel our physical anatomy. He told us that there are regular geometric patterns surrounding the body and that emotionally-triggered disease processes often originate in this invisible web-like network of energy lines, from which they eventually percolate down into the cell structure. (While invisible to ordinary sight, the subtle bodies are easily visible to those who are gifted or trained in that form of intuitive sense-perception known as clairvoyance or "clear-seeing.")

Before ending his impromptu demonstration Father Andrew performed an "adjustment" to the man's energy body, which resulted in the man experiencing an emotional release and a clearing of his physical symptoms. How long the cure lasted I have no idea, but his discomfort had been chronic. Nevertheless, as we all parted company at the end of the evening, the man was still proclaiming his new pain-free status.

So it was that my early investigations led me to a scientific man of God who geometrized with his hands.

The Ancients

Father Andrew was not the first of God's agents to proclaim a connection between Deity and geometry. It is the belief in several eastern cultures that advanced sages or God-men (known as Rishis) brought complete systems of mathematics, geometry, medicine, and so forth and gave them to the early civilizations of Earth. These Rishis are said to have instructed Earth-men in these various disciplines and thus initiated systems of language and scientific knowledge on our planet.

Whatever its origins, the Greeks of Plato's time regarded geometry as being inherent in Nature and the science of geometry as a revelation from God. Plato himself was prompted to declare, "God is a geometer." Over 2,000 years later, in our own century, Albert Einstein echoed the views of Plato with his own observation that "God geometrizes," a position mirrored by another neo-Platonist — Buckminster Fuller — who referred to the triangle as the "signature of God."

Within such disciplines as geomancy and Feng Shui, for example, we learn from the Ancients' legacy about the influence of geometry upon living systems. This legacy of geometry impacting on consciousness stretches back to the annals of ancient Egypt and beyond, where the traditions of sacred geometry sought to incorporate The Divine, The Universal, and The Eternal into the human mind and the human living environment.

Pythagoras was another who maintained that there is an integral union between God, geometry, and consciousness. By 500 BC, his monumental accomplishments were already legendary. He was a true renaissance man, centuries before the term was ever coined. He held that all things, all disciplines — including music, mathematics, geometry, medicine, astronomy, and so forth — are interrelated. His views on such matters are probably best summarized as follows:

"The law of correspondences bridges and unifies all systems of science and philosophy within the singular universal mind of God."

The university which Pythagoras established in Crotona (in southern Italy) combined the secular studies of the sciences together with the sacred studies of the Spirit. His pupils were divided into two groups: the "exoterici," or outer grades, and the "esoterici," who had passed special initiations and were therefore qualified for the inner wisdom teachings. Then, at some appropriate point in their educational process, Pythagoras would introduce his advanced students to the use of geometric designs as a means of effecting an enduring state of expanded consciousness.

Sometime during the late 1930s, a discovery was made which shed additional light on the Pythagorean system of refining consciousness through the use of geometric images. While visiting the library of the Monastery of St. Catherine in Lebanon, Viola Pettit-Neal, Ph.D. (an American professor of oriental religions) found documents which revealed that, for a period of seven years, Pythagoras had had his acolytes focus regularly upon three geometric images: the circle, the cross, and the triangle. As a result, he developed students with greatly enhanced powers of perception on many levels — spiritual as well as intellectual.

Upon her subsequent return to the United States, Dr. Pettit-Neal and her husband Roland, in conjunction with Martha and Walter Burleigh of Tucson, Arizona, developed The Balancing Program. This is a system for expanding one's mental potential, based upon the original consciousness-expanding geometrics of Pythagoras. The program places particular emphasis on balance between the mental and the emotional aspects of consciousness. To date, The Balancing Program has helped hundreds of people reach advanced levels of personal and professional achievement.

Who can say from where Pythagoras gleaned his knowledge of geometrically-induced enlightenment? Perhaps directly from the gods themselves? There appears to be no record of this. What is evident, however, is that from one century to the next, we seem to just go on rediscovering Eternal Truths which we as a species appear to have always known, stemming from somewhere back in our ancestral memory.

Eternal Technology

The practice of employing geometrically generated forcefields as a means of refining consciousness is legendary. This approach, in one form or another, has been utilized for millennia, its universality verified by various cultures in Africa, Asia, Europe, and North America, and for such diverse functions as health care, expanding awareness, and structuring social relationships. From Tibetan monks using intricate mandala patterns for focus and meditation in order to invoke higher states of consciousness, to the Navaho shaman who inscribes medicine wheel drawings upon the ground as part of a healing ritual, geometric-energy technology for enhancing human well-being endures. Geometric wavefields have an inherent authenticity about them which derives from the very fact of their timeless universality.

The eternal frequencies embodied by the IQ Cards have guided human evolution for millennia. They possess the power to catalyze and enhance our innate faculties for intuitive sense-perception or gnosis (direct knowing). This means of knowing was called The Intelligence of The Heart by the ancient Egyptians, and represented a balance of the intuition and the intellect. Even in our modern vernacular we use the term "I know it by heart," suggesting that one has indelibly imprinted certain information in consciousness, either through constant practice and repetition, or through some other agency of memory or recall.

For the early Egyptians, like the Gnostics who followed some centuries later, the Intelligence of the Heart was a function of experiencing one's own *krst* or *christos*, one's internal, heightened state of consciousness. In this context, "knowing through feeling" is a fully valid means of accessing information. These ancient traditions teach us that man is a living temple, embodying cosmic principles and functions which fully equip him for such direct, non-intellectual knowing. It was through the temple training of the Egyptian mystery teachings that the structure of Egyptian science and wisdom was approached through The Intelligence of The Heart.

Yet somewhere along the way, somewhere between classical Egypt and classical physics, intelligence got separated from the heart. Knowing and feeling were divorced. In our male macho-dominated world, we came to only value knowledge which had derived from the force of the intellect. "Feelings" were equated with mushy emotions, "women's intuition," and other such "feminine stuff." And if we wanted to know anything about a person's intelligence, we measured it "scientifically" — with an academically biased, psychologically interpreted IQ (Intelligence Quotient) test.

But now the standard IQ Test for intelligence is suspect. Those who dare to flirt with the heresy of changing current testing methods argue that what we presently measure are the language and arithmetic skills which one has obtained in an affluent Western culture, rather than the true innate intelligence of the individual. By contrast, the Intuition Quotient Cards associated with this book are linked to a period in our evolution of consciousness when intuition and intellect, spirit and matter, were actively acknowledged as aspects of a single reality. I am confident that with our ongoing search for a more universal measure of human potential, we will eventually develop insights about the consciousness of humankind heretofore undreamt of in our present scientific philosophies.

Anthropology recognizes us all as a single species — homo sapiens. All racial groups are thought to have a common ancestry, tracing back to Africa. The Earth's people of all historical and future time periods are bound together by the powerful forces of biochemistry, bio-energetics, and consciousness. Thus, there are genetic factors which we all share, as well as those which make us unique. One of the inherited faculties that we humans share in common — regardless of race or ethnicity — is that of intuitive sense-perception. Everybody's anatomy is naturally wired for intuition. How we choose to use our innate potential is another matter.

Each person's own natural Intuition Quotient (that share or portion of consciousness devoted to direct cognition), is capable of extraordinary accomplishments in receiving, interpreting, and transmitting subtle frequencies, which carry vast amounts of information. So, in our quest for understanding, we must remember that it is equally as important to value one's quotient of intuition, as it is to value one's quotient of intellect. Each embraces a valid form of intelligence, and each is a legitimate — and necessary — means of intelligence-gathering.

2

"Intuition is cosmic fishing.
Once you feel a nibble, you've got to hook the fish."
R. Buckminster Fuller
American architect

CREATING THE IQ CARDS
A Personal Odyssey

OOPS, My Personal Paradigm Is Slipping!

When I departed The University of Maryland with my new, hard won anthropology degree in hand, I felt ready to take on the world. I was scientifically indoctrinated, primed for analytical thinking, and had received a good grade for my studies in mathematical logic. "Surely," I thought, "if there is any additional truth lurking somewhere out there in the world, I now have an academically approved, unshakable framework within which I can comprehend just about anything." But my tightly structured, neatly framed view of reality had not prepared me for what I discovered during my first trip to London, England, about two years after my self-proclaimed undergraduate triumph. On that trip I met naturopathic physicians, spiritual healers, Sanskrit scholars, and yogis with special powers — all of whom spoke confidently about realities of which I had never dreamed. I learned of homeopathy and medical radiesthesia: two techniques of energy medicine which focus on healing via the human energy field. There were even individuals who could recall their own past lives in detail! I sort of expected the guys in the white coats (wielding straight jackets) to come looking for this latter group.

"Have I stepped off into the twilight zone?" I wondered. My concepts of reality were being severely challenged. My carefully constructed, comfortable belief system, reliably grounded in "the scientific method," was beginning to wobble. I had no idea where my internal shakiness would lead. One thing, though, was certain: an unexpected metamorphosis of belief was underway.

Two more years passed. I asked questions, kept an open mind, and I learned. I myself became proficient in radiesthesia and homeopathy. I felt that I was finally finding my own way to honor the higher truths of reality, without either sacrificing my scientific foundations or denying the validity of the new information which I seemed to be constantly uncovering. I had even embarked upon the acquisition of a Ph.D. in psychology, focusing upon the behavioral implications of various energy fields. My project was to investigate those researchers who seemed to have something to contribute to the theory that I had formulated, namely that human behavior is affected in significant ways by a broad spectrum of vibratory phenomena ranging from scientifically measurable magnetic fields to the subtle, unmeasurable forces of homeopathic medicines and thought-energy.

I interviewed and worked with physicians and psychics, chemists and psychologists, physicists and shamans. I felt certain that there was a single, understandable reality which embraced what I knew as science, as well as all this other "far out stuff." So, while residing in the West Indies as my base of operations, I traveled throughout a good part of the Western world, collecting data from experts in their respective fields. Even if those experts were not talking to each other, they had agreed (fortunately for my Ph.D. project) to talk to me. I would later introduce them to each other, so to speak, throughout the pages of my dissertation.

Subtle Energy Geometrics

Shortly after I completed the final work on my doctorate degree in Ohio, I returned to my home base in Barbados and visited my friend Dr. Mark Gallert. Mark was an internationally respected naturopathic physician and a master of psionic or subtle energy technology. When I arrived, Mark was seated at a psionic device of his own design, an elaborate console of dials and switches. He was doing a distant health evaluation of one of his patients back in England. Mark was his customarily affable self and generously allowed my usual barrage of questions about subtle energies. "What's that little card with the circles and lines and what is that instrument you're putting it in?" I queried. "These items," he responded like a tolerant professor, "are the work of Malcolm Rae. He manufactures them back in London. The circles and lines on the cards re-create the energy field of a homeopathic remedy. By inserting the card in this slot of his mag-neto-geometric instrument, I can make a homeopathic remedy and adjust the strength of that remedy to any potency I choose."

Dr. Gallert went on to explain that Malcolm Rae had converted the entire pharmacopoeia of homeo-pathic medicine — over 2,000 remedies — into a precise geometric pattern for each substance. I was truly impressed. Now, in order to create any homeopathic remedy of any strength, all one had to do was simply pop in a geometric card and a vial of plain distilled water, or neutral placebo tablets, turn a dial and wait a few minutes. Normally, such a remedy could have taken hours to create with traditional methods. This was clearly a breakthrough of enormous proportions!

With all my travels and investigations, I thought I had seen a lot — sound frequencies that repaired dam-aged tissues, magnetic fields that instantly stopped bleeding or toothaches, and respected spiritual heal-ers who regularly produced miracle cures. But this was phenomenon of a different order. If Dr. Gallert had told me about Malcolm Rae's magneto-geometrics four years earlier, I would not have appreciated its value. I was still ensconced in my rigid world view. Unyielding skepticism would have blocked my ability to truly hear the import of what he was saying: "a geometric pat-tern drawn to create extremely precise angles of interference produces a selected standing wave or forcefield, corresponding to a specific homeopathic remedy."

I had learned enough about homeopathy to be reasonably well informed on the subject. Traditional homeopathic medicine originated with a German physician, Dr. Samuel Hahnemann, in the late eighteenth century. Homeopathy is founded upon The Law of Similars, or "Like treats like." The Law of Similars states that any substance which can produce certain specific symptoms in a healthy person can cure those same symptoms in a sick person. Homeopathic medicines are administered in extremely small doses and are non-toxic. Homeopathy acts directly upon the underlying energy fields of the body, or the "morphogenetic fields," identified by Dr. Rupert Sheldrake. By conventional methods, a homeopathic remedy could take many painstaking hours to produce. This new Rae technology was a quantum leap beyond that.

At that juncture of my life, skepticism and denial of subtle energy phenomena were no longer options for me. I had passed those barriers several years earlier. However, I was not beyond awe. And that was my reaction to Dr. Gallert's matter-of-fact announcement about the magneto-geometric cards: a stunned, mind-boggling awe.

Subsequently, I set about proving to my own satisfaction that the geometric system of homeopathy actually worked. On numerous occasions, I successfully used the homeopathic remedy cards to effect dramatic healings for myself, family, and friends.

As England held a particular attraction for me as a center for homeopathy and other natural healing methods, I was already in the habit of visiting there as frequently as I could. Thus, within a year of Mark's introducing me to the subtle-energy alchemy of magneto-geometrics, I met Malcolm Rae at his research studios just outside London. He confirmed for me all that I had learned from Dr. Gallert, and more.

Malcolm and I collaborated over a period of several years, and all along I asked him about creating geometric forcefields which corresponded to certain states of consciousness rather than homeopathic remedies. He replied that his personal interest in magneto-geometrics was firmly focused on medical homeopathy. But he encouraged me to extend his pioneering work in geometric technology into the areas of consciousness and psychology, as he was certain that geometrically-produced forcefields for states of consciousness could be created with the same precision as homeopathic ones.

Over the years, since my remarkable meetings with Mark and Malcolm, I have added some variations of my own to their original findings, such as these present IQ Cards. These thirty-six geometric patterns and their corresponding verses are my contribution to the continuing unfoldment of the geometry of consciousness.

3

"I know when I have a problem
and have done all I can to figure it,
I keep listening in a sort of inside silence
'til something clicks and I feel a right answer."

Conrad Hilton
Founder, Hilton Hotels

DOING BUSINESS WITH INTUITION

The Intuitives Are Here

It was a long trek, both in time and experience, from the magneto-geometrics of homeopathy to business gatherings and corporate board rooms. Never in my fondest fantasy would I have imagined such a meeting! And yet here we were, some seventy-odd souls from distant parts of the planet, all convened at the University of Hawaii, in Honolulu. We were attending the world's first "International Conference on Intuitive Decision-Making in Organizations." This was truly a remarkable event.

Was the world now safe for a "closet intuitive" to emerge and openly declare himself among his business peers? And what a variety of human experience we represented! There was a physician from Canada, a businessman from Norway, a university professor from Texas, a chairman of the board from India who spent half his time in Switzerland consulting with corporate heads around the world, a United States Navy lieutenant commander, a management consultant from Holland, a chief of staff for a US senator, and a volleyball coach from San Francisco. What linked us all together was our conviction that something called "intuition" seemed to hold a vast, untapped treasure of creative potential, available to all people, in all areas of human endeavor. We were there to explore different ways of using intuition in business activities. After three days of exchanging and evaluating our various intuitive technologies, we agreed to continue our international meetings. Today the signs bode well for the future of intuition in business.

Still, for some businessmen, the attitude towards intuition is one of skepticism, heavily tinged with resistance to the very idea. By contrast, others in business are quite open to the use of applied intuition in their business life. In fact, I have spoken to high-ranking corporate executives who acknowledge (at least privately) that their outstanding achievements are due to the regular use of intuition. Here, from my own archives, are some examples of applied intuition in the workplace, and use of the IQ Cards for business decision-making:

Intuition In The Corporate Classroom

I stood there facing a whole department of industrial engineers, a group infamous for their use of left brain logic and slide rules. Their department head, Jeff Grayson, was a wonderful guy, but how could I have possibly let him talk me into doing intuition training for such a notoriously linear-thinking group? Surely this was going to be a major exercise in futility! This company was the centerpiece of a Fortune 100 corporate conglomerate, whose operations span the globe. Were these people ready for intuitive decision-making?

I began the program with basic concepts and definitions. A mathematical-like introduction to intuition seemed to warm the cockles of their little engineering hearts and endear me to the group. They became totally attentive to the information and responsive to each intuitive exercise. By the end of the first day, hard core intellectual skeptics had become intuition converts. They realized that they could be both intuitive and linear in their thinking. They would not have to sacrifice one half of their brain for the other. They discovered that, in fact, a balance between the two modes of the mind would actually improve their job performance.

Jeff's department became a happy crucible for grooming creative entrepreneurs who moved on to higher executive positions within the corporation or launched their own private endeavors outside of the company. His was a true classroom for consciousness development, a mecca for intuition and creativity training within a corporate culture.

Teambuilding With Intuition

For over one year the Department of Information Services of a major oil company had been trying to convince their executive board to authorize the purchase of a new $4,000,000 mainframe computer. Their existing technology was not adequate to the demands placed upon it, a situation made worse by growing dissension and severe miscommunication throughout the department. Upper management was not convinced that spending millions on state-of-the-art hardware was the answer to the department's problems. So the department restructured itself: it fired, hired, and shuffled personnel. And still the problems persisted. I was one of a team of consultants who were tackling this massive and complex situation. My particular role was to use applied intuition as a means of teambuilding.

Eventually, after some discussion, we succeeded in obtaining the unanimous agreement of each department manager to support the mainframe proposal. This became the one active project for which they all claimed 100% ownership. We used intuitive troubleshooting to create options, anticipate difficulties, and map strategy. Those who had no "hands on" role in the project were fully aligned in spirit and in consciousness with those who did. New alliances and spontaneous support teams were formed where previously there had been indifference. The department managers coalesced as they never had before. Within four weeks, the project was approved and, shortly thereafter, the new mainframe computer was installed.

Whether your intuitive connection occurs when partnering with colleagues, or when using the IQ Cards for a private decision, refined intuitive skills produce top performance, as well as bottom line results. The

IQ Cards work especially well for those who are committed to guiding their business according to Universal Principles and practical intuition. Typical of the feedback received from a broad cross-section of business people — in varying professions and with differing levels of decision-making authority — are the following comments:

"What I know gets uncovered, and I gain clarity without intellectual filters."

Kathleen Osta, Organizational Development Consultant

"The IQ Cards stimulate creative thinking that carries a calm, spiritual quality."

Renee Panakia, Executive VP & COO, Financial Services

"... A reusable tool for achieving clarity — especially for business issues. The verses speak to you about the direction your actions should take."

Nicolette Lemmon, President/Owner, Marketing Agency

"The Cards provide a dramatically effective way to access deep levels of insight. The interaction of group members heightens the quality of the intuitive connections we are able to make."

Richard and Chrystal Otto, President and CEO, Educational Psychology

"... For me, the geometric pattern began to pulsate — it triggered my answer in the form of a visual image."

Douglas Felkins, Owner, Landscaping Company

"In response to my question, the IQ Cards accurately predicted coming contract complications. I was much better prepared for the situation, having focused (using the Cards) before the meeting."

Dr. Sandra E. Howlett, Corporate Trainer, Human Resources

Business, like all other areas of human endeavor, is but a stage upon which we get to experience the quality of our own consciousness. We act upon decisions we make which, in turn, mirror back to us the skillfulness of our actions and the depth of our knowing. The IQ Cards provide a systematic means of reviewing the content of our own consciousness, even before we act. Because the IQ Cards incorporate universal principles as an element of decision-making, they naturally enhance our *direct cognition* or *intuitive sense-perception.* The Cards are analogous to training wheels for a bicycle, but in this case, you are learning to master the fine balance between intuition and intellect that is required to operate from The Intelligence of The Heart. Using a different analogy, the IQ Card acts much like a musical tuning fork, aligning and entraining one's consciousness to "play the right note" in dealing with a particular issue.

4

*"When the ears of the student are ready to hear, then
cometh the lips to fill them with wisdom."*

Hermes Trismegistus
mystic teacher of early Egypt
circa 21st century BC

PRINCIPLES OF
INTUITIVE KNOWING

Knowing What Is

The various schools of intuitive investigation
emphasize different components of the intuitive process, depending upon their own sets of values and
priorities. In this section, I offer some guiding principles
which I have found most helpful in comprehending
intuition.

The IQ Cards, like the Chinese *I Ching* and the
Viking Runes, reflect a flow of basic, universal forces
moving throughout the situation upon which one is
focusing. The IQ Cards reveal to us knowledge and
wisdom which we already carry within our own inner
consciousness.

Indeed, the very essence of *intuitive intelligence* is
perceiving the energy of *what is*. With every situation,
problem, person, group, organization, or nation, there

is an *"isness,"* a characterizing field of energy which establishes identity with the precision of a fingerprint. This "isness" represents the *truth of the current dynamic,* which is not always captured by the five senses, by appearances, or by the reasoning power of logic. Perhaps there *are* times when "what you see is what you get," but personally, I am doubtful. My view is that unless both intuition and intellect are working together as a balanced, harmonious unit, some essential truth about the "isness" of an individual or a situation gets lost. The perceiver becomes prey to illusion surrounding that which is perceived, the mind unwittingly seduced and entrained by the dominance of symptom and effect. Or put differently, as Ralph Waldo Emerson once expressed it to a certain 19th century ego-maniac, " … don't bother to tell me who you are because what you are shouts so loudly I cannot hear what you are saying." Many years of intuitive investigations have led me to the view that the question is frequently as important as the answer. A little philosophical limerick occurred to me as a way of illustrating this point:

The Situation As Guru

A seeker: "How would you know
             upon what to decide,
             when truth does so
             elusively hide?"

A wise one: "But ah, my friend,
             there is no mystery,
             for the answer lies
             in the question, you see.

Just look about you,
to what you attract;
therein lies the information
you appear to lack."

"The situation as guru" means that whatever situation or issue stands before you in this moment, that is your teacher, your guru. As a perennial student of philosophy and the main protagonist of my own life's dramas, I have come to believe that the answers we seek in life are contained within the situations we attract to ourselves. This is a view around which my understanding continually unfolds. Thus, it was most instructive for me to discover a similar point of view expressed from an Eastern perspective. In Grumukie, the language of prayer of the Sikh religious tradition, GU=darkness and RU=light. Thus, "guru" is understood to be that which moves one's consciousness from darkness to light.

The situation as guru calls upon the individual to skillfully make decisions and choices within the parameters set by the current situation. Like that part of the American Indian's vision quest, where insights and answers are discovered along the path that the questor walks, so too are the situations in our life constantly inviting us to use them as cues for greater inner clarity as vehicles for expanding our awareness. There are times, for example, when the darkness of a certain circumstance catalyzes the light of self-discovery and creative breakthrough — for the individual as well as an entire group. Under such conditions, decision-making through intuitive intelligence becomes its own ever-expanding reward.

The Principle Of Resonance

Even without the intention or awareness of our conscious-mind, *the principle of resonance* remains in constant operation, attracting to ourselves events and circumstances which help us grow by holding before us a reflection of our own state of being. Mirroring is one way that we come to acknowledge our true responsibility for acting in accordance with our own highest inner guidance. At any level of social organization — the individual, the couple, the company, the nation, or the group of nations — *the mirror's the thing that speaks most profoundly to our inner hearing.*

We may not always like what we see when we look into our particular situational mirror, but the images we find there invariably reflect some aspect — beautiful or revolting — of our own consciousness. We do have options on how best to respond to our mirrored images. We may attempt to deny and destroy their unyielding existence. Or we can meet their steady gaze with a compassionate, unifying embrace of light and oneness: healing old wounds, making all things new, ascending to new plateaus of creative accomplishment.

However much the factors of mirroring and subtle causation may escape our intellectual comprehension, the eternal principles of *affinity* and *resonance*, and *cause* and *effect* remain operative in the universe and in the affairs of humankind. Consider the view that whatever is the current situation commanding your attention — be it "positive" or "negative" — it is present in your life in order to support the *expansion* of your awareness and not your *contraction* into the confines of limited perception. Should a given situation not look very supportive to you, remember that some of us are often brought to wisdom and understanding kicking and screaming all the way. Isn't it comforting to know that there are universal forces leading us to clarity, in spite of what we do? It is as though we humankind are junior trainees, learning to make better decisions under the coaching — sometimes benign and sometimes tough — of Higher Intelligence.

Our challenge, then, is to see beyond the drama and effect, however fair or foul it may appear. Our lesson is to master the skill of *balanced perception*, neither capitulating with failure nor growing arrogant with success: to treat success and failure — those two impostors — just the same. The mandate of our innermost mind is to comprehend the wisdom contained within the problem — to understand, via The Intelligence of the Heart, what our consciousness is really saying to us through the situation as it presents itself.

Intuitive Mind-Directed Selection

The IQ Cards are a tool for self-counseling via direct intuitive perception, allied with your common sense. The Cards systematically reflect the dynamics of your own consciousness. This intentional and disciplined use of intuitive intelligence for making choices is what I call *Intuitive Mind-Directed Selection*. With this approach, you consciously employ your intuitive mind in conjunction with an external tool or method of some kind — in this instance the selection of an IQ Card.

Intuitive Mind-Directed Selection is founded upon the principles of Cosmic Law. The Japanese spiritual tradition of Johrei recognizes a *Divine Law of Order.* The Law of Order states that everything in the universe — molecules, man, and planet — has its proper place in the scheme of things, whether it is a blade of grass or an entire nation.

The Law of Order suggests that all things and all events are governed by structure and *Universal Intelligence*, and not by randomness or accident; that each of us attracts our own unique situations, whether or not we are consciously aware of it; and that whether it is the IQ Card you select, the individual you choose to marry, or the current compelling issue which stands before you, there are no "accidents." Using the instructions given in this book, the IQ Card you select may speak to your issue on various planes of reality: physical, emotional, transpersonal, and so on. Remain open and receptive in order to hear and interpret the deeper message. The Kybalion, an ancient book of Hermetic Wisdom, puts it this way: *"Chance is but a name for Law not recognized; there are many planes of causation, but nothing escapes the Law* (of Order). *"* My study of various wisdom teachings concerning divine causation and human perception leads me to the conclusion that there are no accidents in the universe — only the workings of Natural Law, imperfectly understood by humankind.

Informed Intuition

Informed Intuition means inner knowing and intellect working together in tandem. It means drawing upon all that you are, right brain and left ... spirit, mind, and body. This principle refers to a state of awareness — indeed a state of *readiness* for decision-making. It requires that one have the fullest available range of accurate information — intuitive as well as intellectual — when making a decision to take action. Informed Intuition is made possible by one's Extended Range of Perception (EROP), and involves multi-sensory input, i.e. data that may be received via multiple channels: the physical senses, deductive/inductive reasoning, feelings, and direct perception. This is full-spectrum consciousness. The highest quality of *Intuitive Intelligence* relies upon one's Informed Intuition or Extended Range of Perception: no relevant information from any source is excluded. Decisions and actions deriving from such a state of awareness embody both wisdom and practicality. Or, as one of my colleagues put it, "intuition is the guide that leads the intellect to the place it needs to think." Intuition, then, focuses insight upon our true priorities, while the intellect is best used to manage the logistics necessary for implementing the insight which intuition has provided.

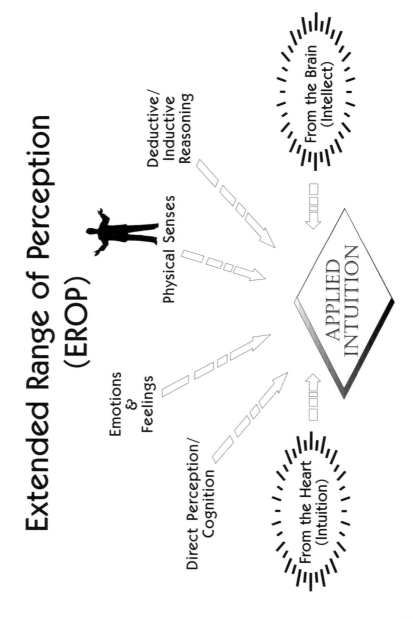

Extended Range of Perception (EROP)

5

"Intuition is the code word for global transformation."
Dr. Willis Harman, President
Institute of Noetic Sciences

LISTENING TO YOURSELF

Modes Of Action

About 2,500 years ago in ancient China, Lao Tsu (a contemporary of Confucius) recorded his own teachings in a work which we know today as the Tao Te Ching. The Tao (pronounced "dow"), as it is popularly called, consists of explanations of the natural order of things and instructions on how to consciously conduct our lives in accordance with natural law. My understanding is that the spirit of the Tao is about human consciousness moving in harmony with the rhythms of Universal Intelligence in any given situation.

The accompanying thirty-six geometric patterns and verses bear a kinship to the principles of Lao Tsu's Tao. The IQ Cards provide a structure for tapping your innate intuitive faculty. They serve as "training wheels," until you feel steady enough to direct your finely tuned vehicle of intuitive sense-perception in whatever direction you may choose. Even after you have become skilled in intuitive decision-making, the IQ Cards will serve as a reference source when you need an "intuition tune-up" from time to time. Remember that a fundamental purpose of the IQ Cards is to help you hear your own inner wisdom more clearly. For whatever specific issue or concern you may have, the IQ Cards prompt you to activate your Intuitive Intelligence. This enhances the quality of your decision-making.

There are three *modes of action* into which the thirty-six IQ Cards are divided — twelve cards in each group. As in the spirit of the Tao, the fundamental idea behind these three modes of action is to focus and fine-tune the direction of your attention. This focus and fine-tuning leads you naturally and effortlessly to a course of *purposeful action*. In this context, purposeful action occurs when your actions are in alignment with your life purpose and your values ... when you act from The Intelligence of The Heart.

The three modes of action are generally described as follows:

Direct, Overt Action: Numbers D1 Through D12

This is action characterized by timely, hands on, proactive intervention in a given situation. Physical, three-dimensional activity is usually indicated here. Your intuitive focus guides you easily to plan, to implement, to follow through, or to get involved. For example, you may have been inwardly aware for some time that your association with a particular individual is toxic, destructive, and unlikely to improve without a major shift of some kind. But, until now, you have simply endured the discomfort and done nothing. IQ Card D2, "Gifts of The Grail Expressed," could be saying to you "Act now on what you already know you need to do with respect to this relationship: speak your mind, share your feelings, make your move — whatever it needs to be — now."

Listening and Receiving: Numbers L1 through L12

This is action characterized by inner listening to that "still small voice." Your focus is on gaining more information, insight, clarity, balance, or patience. This is the state of "actionless action" referred to by the sages. You consciously choose patience — to wait — to allow the natural rhythms of the Universe to move, at their own rate, into greater harmony with the issue at hand.

Perhaps there have been instances when you thought that the time was right and that you had all the relevant information you needed to take a particular action. So you acted, only to be reminded later on that had you been more patient, more willing to listen and to "live in the question," you would have saved yourself considerable time, money, or discomfort. If, for example, before making your move, you had selected IQ Card L7, "Inspired Insight," you would have known that rational thought alone was insufficient for taking action. You would have been aware that profound causal forces were in motion around your issue. Perhaps then you would have been more patient in waiting for Divine timing, and in following your deeper guidance on the matter.

Higher Order Creativity: Numbers H1 through H12

This is action characterized by higher-mind influences, by engaging the faculties of creativity, vision, and intuitive intelligence. You attune your sensing faculty to the loving presence of the muse. Or to a guardian spirit of Light. Or to an angelic presence that infuses you with love and wisdom. You consciously bring your intuitive sense-perception to focus upon and to shape physical realities.

I know several people who consciously receive guidance from loving spirit beings who are present with the individual. This guidance comes from angelic, Christed, Masters of Light and Love, who do not deceive. Through inner visualization, direct visual contact, extended hearing, or other means of direct perception, these human individuals communicate with advanced intelligences on matters of day-to-day earthly importance. But there are times when the Earth-bound communicator, for whatever reasons, chooses to rationalize, to ignore, or to otherwise tune out the celestial messengers of Higher Order Creativity. IQ Card H6, "Guardians Of Light," invites the individual to step out into greater conscious knowing, using the intuitive capacity which the individual already possesses. The mode of Higher Order Creativity is concerned with intentionally uniting the finite experience of one's personality with the infinite reality of one's Higher Self.

Turning Up The Volume

Note the key phrase, "characterized by," in each of the three definitions listed above. While it is recommended to focus upon a single mode of action, it is clearly possible to have two or even all three modes of action operating (in tandem, in sequence, or in some other cooperative fashion) on a given issue. This is simply a reminder not to over-focus on a single mode of action to the exclusion of the others. For example, there are instances when a D card may automatically engage your faculties of Higher Order Creativity or produce within you a Listening/Receiving response. Remember that the IQ Cards serve you by turning up the volume of your "still small voice" within, so that your actions become aligned with the natural rhythms of Universal Intelligence which flow through your daily affairs.

Getting Your Own Cues

There is no one perfect way to respond to the IQ Cards. Individual reactions vary widely and each person's experience is appropriate to him/herself at the time it occurs. For example, at one end of the response spectrum, there are those who report major shifts in their perception. They actually see subtle energy fields produced by the geometric pattern, such as flashing lights, colors, or moving waveforms. Others report pronounced new insights into long-standing issues, incredible memory recall, and clear anatomical signals — all associated with focusing on the IQ Cards. In contrast, still others have responses to the Cards that are equally telling but far less dramatic than the previous group. Their cues are subtle — a quiet tingling, a minor twitching, a mild nudge of feeling — soft signals that are more like a whisper than a shout, and yet lack nothing in precision. Then there are those who seem to experience nothing — no visual impressions, no spontaneous ideas, no physical signals — nothing. It is important to remember that for some individuals the effect of the IQ cards may not be felt immediately. There are those who will require a little more time to become sensitized to the cards' subtle frequencies.

Whatever response you may have, know that there is no need for alarm should your body spontaneously react in some way to these geometric forcefields. These are automatic neurological responses, analogous to the ear's reaction to a ringing telephone, or the nose's response to fragrance. Any one or several of your faculties of sense-perception may become sensitized with heightened receptivity, as a result of your exposure to the IQ cards.

Nor is the presence or absence of an immediate sensory response to the cards to be taken as an absolute indication of their effectiveness in refining intuitive perception. There are delayed reactions. Indeed, there are many unseen subtleties within the realm of possibility, as we train ourselves to extend normal perception into the higher frequencies of matter and mind. With The Intelligence of The Heart as our guide, there is no cause for fright or upset as we start to feel and know more of the invisible realities which surround us.

To further facilitate your responsiveness to the signals of inner guidance, whenever possible join with others in working through your intuitive decision-making process. Share insights. Support each other by profoundly listening — with all of your faculties. Hear what the person's *being,* as well as his words, are saying — it is instructive to recognize inconsistencies when they occur. This kind of person-to-person cooperation is fun, empowering, and tends to improve the precision of your intuitive insight. Higher quality answers and resolutions usually result when working with others.

It is recommended that everyone in your support/ training group share a common commitment to truly listen and speak "from the heart." It is usually neither helpful nor pleasant to pursue intuitive decision-making with those who reject intuition, deny their own knowing, or otherwise limit themselves to only a mental, intellectual understanding of reality.

Common Response Patterns

While each person's intuitive response mechanism is uniquely his/her own, there are some recurring patterns that we have observed to be linked to the use of the IQ Cards:

Contemplation: For some, the Card's forcefield seems to induce a sense of reverie and meditation. This state of mind may also be accompanied by feelings of relaxation, relief, and lowering of both physical and emotional tensions.

Eagerness: There is an excitement and a kind of "can do" elation that many experience in response to the IQ forcefield. It is as if they have discovered a long-sought-after treasure, or at least the "road map" that promises to lead them to that treasure.

Physical Sensations: Physical sensations are a common response. Feelings of "things shifting and realigning" in various parts of the body frequently occur. There are also certain specific anatomical physical responses which constantly repeat for some individuals. These often turn out to be intuitive cues, the body's way of alerting one's conscious mind to the presence of information being generated by one's higher mind. Physical sensations in particular areas of the body may also indicate specific patterns of consciousness that require clearing or release. In some instances, this could point to a precise correspondence between a physical "symptom" and its cause in consciousness.

Clarity: The experience of clarity can occur in various ways. For some it is a subtle, almost mystical, feeling sensation that is difficult to describe. It is as if cobwebs, doubts, and shadows have generally been swept from their minds. Others say that they feel more confident, determined, committed, and focused on whatever is their priority or chosen life path. Still others mention spontaneous thoughts that come with lightning speed, clearly and unexpectedly. Ideas just pop into their heads, from "right out of the blue."

Depth of Feeling: At times, deep feelings arise when one aligns with an IQ Card forcefield. The character of the feeling can range across a whole continuum of possibilities from isolation to union, from frustration to fulfillment ... there is an entire spectrum of possible emotional nuances. But whatever their form, these feelings are distinguished from others by a sense of profundity and pertinence. We sense their depth and "rightness" for the situation. Often neither the origin nor the meaning of these feelings are adequately understood at the time.

A Presence: Some particularly sensitive individuals describe what they call "a presence" in the room when using the IQ Cards. Such presences are felt as being positive, loving, supportive, and uplifting. Some persons say that they experience this energy presence as angelic. Here is a summary of an account given by an especially competent individual who researched the IQ Cards and who routinely deals with subtle, intuitive states of consciousness:

> *"In using several of the IQ Cards together to create an etheric environment, I became aware of the presence of five devic spirits representing Air, Fire, Water, and Earth, and standing in the center was Wood — [a] living tree spirit, rooted into the earth, reaching up into heaven. The devas communicated that their mission is to materialize spaces for dimensional attunement that can be accepted by a wide range of humans ... this is one way of helping to bring about the higher mind connection."*

New Areas of Challenge: A common report following the use of the IQ Cards is that of new growth challenges arising in one's life. It seems that the IQ forcefields have a way of disturbing the *status quo* when one's consciousness is locked in a state of misalignment. What follows is a rare and particularly dramatic example of how the IQ Card forcefields can dislodge misqualified energies within a person's consciousness:

There was a teacher of the Oriental energy-healing arts, a sensitive, spiritual person: much revered, widely respected, and deservedly so. On one occasion, I exposed the teacher to an etheric environment created by four IQ Cards. The teacher's immediate response to the IQ Card energies was that they were "... calming ... deeply relaxing ... even blissful ... very powerful ... in all my many years of energy-healing, I've never experienced anything like this ... it creates the smell of perfume ... I see lights and colors around the IQ geometric ... there is a sound, a tone coming from the cards." When he and I spoke again the following day, he would have nothing more to do with the IQ Cards, stating that as he was driving home after his initial pleasant response, a dark, menacing cloud hovered around him. He seemed to attribute this to some defect in the IQ Cards. What the teacher failed to realize, however, was that — with all his legitimate, well-earned spiritual attainment — there were still areas of his consciousness that were ripe for refinement and further advancement. Much like the action of a homeopathic remedy that triggers the release of toxins from the body, the IQ Cards had simply served him by stirring up some of his own mental toxicity that was ready for release from his consciousness. Unfortunately, the teacher had drawn an incorrect conclusion from his experience and projected fault onto the IQ Cards.

So when you engage the IQ Cards, it would not be surprising to find breakthroughs, unexpected opportunities, new personal abilities, serendipitous occurrences, the highlighting of dysfunctional personal stuff — the good along with the bad — moving quickly to the surface for appropriate and timely handling. And with all that goes on during this transition period, there is an increased ease of manifestation — not always of exactly what you thought you were going to manifest, but certainly in the direction of your highest good.

Nothing: There are those who say that they feel nothing in response to the IQ Card forcefields. For some this lack of response happens on their first few exposures to the Cards, until they become more sensitized to subtle forcefields. Many receive benefit from the verse, without the geometric. Should you feel, say, after three months or more of regular use, that you receive no benefit from the IQ Cards, we recommend that you pass them along to someone else who can make use of them.

There is nothing "wrong" with anyone who experiences nothing with the IQ Cards. We recognize that this approach to refining intuitive sense-perception will not suit everyone, and that there are many other valid paths to intuitive knowing. So if the IQ Cards — for whatever reason — do not work for you, you have not failed. It could simply mean that this particular method is not for you at this time. Investigate other methods. But whatever you do, do not give up your quest for clear intuitive knowing. It is your birthright.

6

*"The evolution of the human mind ... depends upon the
evolution of intuition and reason ... Intuition is an
innate quality, but it can be developed and cultivated."*
Dr. Jonas Salk

HOW TO USE THE IQ CARDS

This chapter focuses on two techniques for using
the IQ Cards: "Technique A: Seven Aspects" offers a
flexible structure for intuitive decision-making on any
given issue; "Technique B: Correspondences In Consciousness" provides guidance based upon behavioral
symptoms or patterns.

Technique A: Seven Aspects

In facilitating intuitive decision-making via the IQ
Cards, for individuals and for groups, I have come to
identify several fundamental steps or stages in the
process of consulting one's own inner knowing. These
measures, or "Seven Aspects," as I call them, represent a minimal structure for intuitive decision-making.
They are intended to help you cut through your own
blockages and resistances and move with elegance right
to the core of an issue, to deal with it. The Seven Aspects
are:

1. Define Your Issue

2. Seek Divine Indifference

3. Listen Intuitively

4. Own Your Impressions

5. Make Your Decision

6. Take Purposeful Action

7. Honor YourSelf

Consider these seven areas of information, not as a rigid technical blueprint, but rather as a flexible schematic diagram, pointing the way through intuitive territory. Refer to them, as necessary, along your decision-making journey. At times, it may be most appropriate to start with Aspect #1 and move sequentially through #7. At other times, the beginning point could be anywhere along the continuum from 1 to 7, and all you need at that point is to refer to some part of the guidelines as a reminder. In any event, practice with the IQ Cards and the Seven Aspects will strengthen and refine your innate intuitive ability. What follows is an elaboration upon these Seven Aspects, and instructions for using the IQ Cards. Have a pad and pen handy. Sometimes a tape recorder could also be useful.

Aspect #1: Define Your Issue

The first thing to do when utilizing intuitive intelligence for decision-making is to define your issue as clearly as you can. Define your issue with all the insight, precision, and integrity that you have at your command. The intellect has a role here, for it is the clarity of your assessment of the situation, or the insightfulness of your questions, which attracts to itself a corresponding clarity of answer and resolution. You may consider an issue as being either positive or negative in nature. Not all issues are problems. There are times when the words "challenge" or "opportunity" might more accurately define what is really happening in a situation. Be as thoughtful, accurate, and concise as possible.

Defining Your Issue

✧ Write down your definition. It is helpful to review your written issue several times.

✧ Rewrite your issue, as you feel inclined, reducing the statement to as few words as possible.

✧ Capture the core or causal concerns, rather than just settling on symptoms which are easily identified.

An example of defining an issue according to symptoms might be: "My boss is indifferent to my work and insensitive to me as an individual. Most people at work don't like him because he just makes our lives miserable." Looking at the same situation from a more causal perspective, the following questions might be raised: "Am I aligned with my life's purpose in my present job? How might I feel more fulfilled in my work? What is the most appropriate way to resolve the resentment I feel towards my boss?"

Aspect #2: Seek Divine Indifference

The key to making an Intuitive Mind-Directed Selection is to put "attachment to outcomes" aside. Assume the detached attitude which some sages describe as Divine Indifference: the willingness to be guided from within only by the highest source of Universal Intelligence, regardless of what the mundane drama looks like.

Seeking Divine Indifference

✧ Still your mind.

✧ Take several deep breaths and relax.

✧ Feel yourself moving into a state of calm, centered awareness. You are open, alert, and receptive for whichever ideas or impressions might present themselves.

✧ You feel detached, yet very present. You are anticipating but not anxious. There is a fine balance of your consciousness here, as you intentionally position your mind to idle upon the threshold between conscious and unconscious perception. This is the state of awareness from which an intuitive-mind directed selection is made.

✧ Slowly sort through the thirty-six IQ Cards, *without reading them.*

✧ Allow your inner guidance to direct your fingers in selecting one card.

✧ Note the letter D, L, or H indicating the preferred *mode of action*, as explained earlier. This is a reminder of the importance of the mode of action in helping to set the tone of your eventual course of action. You may want to reread the section on "Modes Of Action," to become more familiar with the three primary modes.

Aspect #3: Listen Intuitively

Listening Intuitively

✧ Read the text of the selected IQ Card, being aware of all ideas, impressions, or "aha"s that are stimulated by the verse.

✧ Do any words or phrases stand out?

✧ Does the message of the Card speak to your issue or your area of decision-making in some way? If so, how?

✧ Jot down the message received.

✧ Does the message you receive from the IQ Card's verse come to you from what is written, or do you perceive something that is implied or unwritten — something "between the lines?"

✧ Do you recognize some particular theme that applies to you?

✧ Is there a particular awareness or memory triggered within you? If so, just make a note of it. If you have no such impressions, that too is all right.

✧ Focus on the Card's geometric pattern. Place the Card in an upright position twelve to eighteen inches away, at eye level. For the sake of clarity, briefly recall your issue and then release it; do not dwell on it.

⬦ As you focus, let it be with an open mind and an open heart. The necessary insight will flow of its own accord and in its own time. Remember, the formula for working with the IQ geometric is: Focus — Open — Receive.

⬦ Hold a steady gaze on the pattern for about three to five minutes. Be attentive, receptive, and poised for perception, but *without expectations*.

⬦ Be aware of all feelings, thoughts, visions, or impressions that occur as you are focused on the pattern.

⬦ Note any physical shifts that occur within or around your body. **Censor nothing.**

⬦ Give free reign to the flow of your open intuitive sense-perception, noting the nuances that move within your awareness.

And should you experience or feel absolutely nothing, don't fret. Your reaction to the Card is an individual matter. There is no "wrong" response.

You may choose to alternate your focus between the geometric side and the verse side of the card, depending on where you seem to have the most significant response or insight. Spend no more than five to seven minutes on Aspect #3 at any one time. Keeping the time frame short helps to optimize a spontaneous flow of creative insight.

Aspect #4: Own Your Impressions

Honor your inner experiences, even if they do not immediately make sense to you. Remember that intuitive insight often comes very quickly and in flashes, and it can speak volumes within seconds. So don't censor, "edit," or deny your experiences. Instead capture them as brief notes or drawings, or speak them into a tape recorder as they occur. All that you experience during intuitive listening is important — visions, memories, thoughts, feelings, sensations, impressions — everything. Acknowledge what happens and record it in some form.

When you consider all of the insights and impressions catalyzed by both sides of the IQ Card, do you come to an obvious resolution — complete or partial —for your issue?

Aspect #5: Make Your Decision

Making Your Decision

✧ Set your intentions. What is the condition or situation you are intending to create through your decision?

✧ How do you want to feel, in carrying out that decision?

✧ Make your decision using all the best information — intuitive and intellectual — that you now have at your disposal, based upon your understanding and clarity at this time.

✧ Decide on a course of action which resonates with The Intelligence of Your Heart.

Such a decision will be absent of all ill intent. No blame or guilt is assigned. It is fun and joyful. And it also naturally aligns with the highest good for yourself and your family or organization. This way everyone wins every time, regardless of the risk or the magnitude of the issue.

Aspect #6: Take Purposeful Action

Purposeful action is characterized by its alignment with your life purpose and values. If a given action truly coincides with your individual life purpose, it will usually also agree with the purpose of your particular group or organization. At a feeling level, purposeful action just "feels right." It isn't something you can always articulate. You just know it's the "right" thing to do, or not do, as the case may be.

Taking Purposeful Action

✧ Having now reached a decision on a course of action for your issue, how will you nourish and sustain your inner motivation to see that the issue is harmoniously resolved?

✧ What kind of support systems — personal and/or logistical — are necessary in order to help you maintain your commitment to action?

✧ Are all roles and responsibilities defined clearly, for carrying out your decision(s)? Identify specific goals which will help you implement your decision.

✧ Have you considered strategy and timing?

✧ What additional information might you need?

✧ How will you monitor the results of your actions?

Write down or record all newly generated information, insights, and questions which could impact upon your actions in any way.

Aspect #7: Honor YourSelf

Honoring YourSelf

✧ Be in the present.

✧ In light of your new insights, review the current status of the original issue. Acknowledge that which is clear and true for you in this moment.

✧ What obvious, self-evident truths now stand out to you more clearly?

✧ Up to this point in this exercise, what has been most meaningful for you?

✧ Are further decisions still pending, or additional actions required? Perhaps even more clarity can be gained by moving through the Seven Aspect Cycle again, with your new insights factored into your definition of the issue.

✧ Celebrate your breakthroughs of awareness. Acknowledge the shifts in your own consciousness. Recognize when the old issue is no more because your perception of it, your decisions, and your actions have rendered it moot or resolved it into a higher order of challenge.

✧ Take a moment to savor your success, and to appreciate the inner resources which made it possible. Feel the "rightness" of the results, and notice the richness you experience from using *both* your intuition and your intellect.

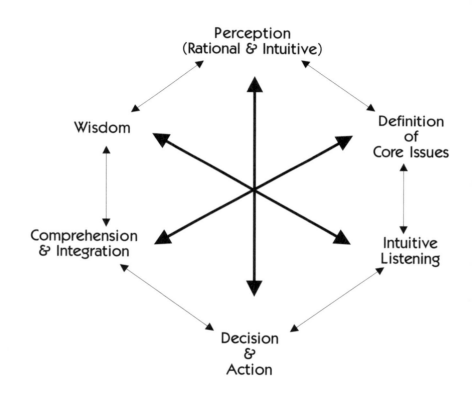

**APPLIED INTUITION
DECISION-MAKING PROCESS**

Technique B: Correspondences In Consciousness

All of us have patterns in our consciousness which predispose us to certain modes of thought and behavior. Sometimes we choose to act in ways that produce fun, freedom, and growth, while other choices bring us pain, fear, and constriction. Even though we may not recognize the presence or the origin of our subtle behavioral tendencies, nevertheless they are with us, influencing the circumstances of our life.

Later in this section, there is a list of fifteen categories of correspondences. These correspondences relate specific patterns in consciousness to their complementary IQ Card forcefields. The patterns in consciousness represented here are ones which, when resolved, tend to open us up to more joy and abundance in life. The intention of the chart is to provide a quick, general point of reference for matching the IQ Cards with identified issues or problems.

This is an effective exercise for using the Cards. It takes about 10–12 minutes:

1. From the list, note that each condition or pattern-in-consciousness shows two corresponding IQ Cards. The first Card listed in each category is the primary or lead Card. The second Card listed is the secondary or anchor Card.

2. Choose the condition/pattern-in-consciousness which you feel most closely describes your situation. Select the primary and secondary Cards. Place the lead card directly in front of you, within twenty-four inches of the center of your forehead.

The IQ Card should be placed so that you can comfortably view the geometric pattern.

3. Hold an easy steady gaze on the lead Card for about five minutes. Be aware of everything you experience during this period: insights, ideas, body responses, feelings, etc.

4. Read the card's verse.

5. Relax and allow about one minute for the integration of your experience.

6. Next, focus on the secondary or anchor card for about five minutes, as described above in steps (2) and (3).

7. Then read the verse of this secondary card, as in step (4).

8. Now take a minute or so to integrate this second experience. Then make notes on all of your insights, experiences, impressions, thoughts, etc. that occurred during this exercise.

9. What conclusions, if any, do you draw? What action, if any, do you now feel inclined to take? Lovingly implement appropriate action(s) according to your clearest perception.

NOTE: How quickly patterns in consciousness change will vary from one person to the next. Even within a single individual's life, the amount of time required for change may differ from one period to another, so be at peace within yourself. There are several variables which determine how fast change will occur: intensity of desire, willingness, clarity of perception, attachment to cherished outcomes, deeply rooted genetic memory, and so on. Some individuals experience profound shifts in consciousness in the course of doing the exercise, whereas for others changes occur over hours, days, weeks, or months. Thus, it is important to frequently monitor your internal reality for shifts in feeling, attitude, and perception. It is equally important to observe the immediate events and the relationships in your life, so that you know how the Universe is mirroring back to you the shifts you are making inside yourself.

SPECIAL NOTE: These IQ Geometric Forcefields have the capacity to dislodge energies within your consciousness that are not aligned with your true Soul-self. There may be occasions when misaligned or misqualified energy patterns are uprooted and exposed: menacing thoughts, feelings, and images posturing as reality. **This is nothing to fear — it is part of your liberation process**. Treat these energies as toxins of mind, body, or spirit that are ready for clearing and release. If uncomfortable feelings/symptoms/experiences persist, seek the services of a loving, competent professional who understands spirit-mind-body inter-relationships. Should you need additional insight or want to secure information about available resources, please refer to the Appendix for instructions.

Condition/Pattern-in-Consciousness	Complementary IQ Cards	
1. Distracted; scattered; need for focus and grounding	D4	Grounding Esoteric Energies
	H12	Sun Phase
2. Victimhood, lack of accepting responsibility; need to be more consciously at cause and proactive with respect to one's own life	H4	Miracles of Compassion
	D11	Higher-Self Discipline
3. Insecurity, feelings of inadequacy or rejection; need for the security of the Self.	H4	Miracles of Compassion
	H8	The Will to Harmonize
4. Stuffing emotions; need to harmoniously express feelings	H10	Abundance Without Resistance
	D12	Sacred/Secular Synthesis
5. Tendency to carry guilt, self denial, accepting all blame; need to forgive self and others	L5	Knowing Through Feeling
	D9	Life Force

Condition/Pattern-in-Consciousness		Complementary IQ Cards
6. Overtaxing one's self, tendency to self-overload; need to unburden, to unlock one's own joyful flow	H6	Guardians of Light
	D8	Renewal
7. Involvement in abusive relationships; need to refine the quality of relationships one attracts	D10	Fertile Expansion
	H11	Space Perceptions
8. Unreleased ancient pain, long-standing hurt and bitterness; need to release and forgive, and to focus on potentializing the present moment	H2	Primal Yin
	D5	Gaia Growth
9. Resisting one's own Higher Self; need for openness and receptivity to one's own growth and knowing	L7	Inspired Insight
	D4	Grounding Esoteric Energies
10. Anger, confusion, reactionary behavior; need for the awareness of truth in given situations	L5	Knowing Through Feeling
	H12	Sun Phase

Condition/Pattern-in-Consciousness	Complementary IQ Cards
11. Need to expand one's personal sense of power and sense of centeredness	H8 The Will to Harmonize H10 Abundance Without Resistance
12. Self condemnation; need for the exaltation of one's eternal God-self	D10 Fertile Expansion H8 The Will to Harmonize
13. Emotional attachments, dysfunctional cherished outcomes; need for clear internal (*intra*-personal) and *inter*-personal communications	D8 Renewal H11 Space Perceptions
14. Need to experience the universe as totally loving and supportive at all times and under all circumstances	D12 Sacred/Secular Synthesis H8 The Will to Harmonize
15. Need to allow one's self that which nourishes the soul, those environments and experiences which recognize and cultivate one's truest essence	D9 Life Force o v e H10 Abundance Without Resistance

7

*"The lines of evidence point to a study of consciousness
...what I prefer to call "noetics." In order to understand ...we will have to abandon many conventional
concepts. We must be prepared to reject the very
foundations of contemporary science, if need be, in
order to understand what we are now seeing."*

Dr. Edgar D. Mitchell
US Astronaut
Founder, Institute of Noetic Sciences

APPLICATIONS UNLIMITED

Are You Getting What You Intended?

The IQ Cards are designed to be flexible: applicable
to a wide range of human situations where the input
of intuitive intelligence is desired. The Cards are also
cross-cultural in scope, since the subtle aligning influence of the forcefields bypasses our reliance upon
language and ethnicity.

The listing of applications given in this chapter is
not meant to be exhaustive. As our individual lives are
continually evolving, and the variety of human experience is broad, we expect that variations on ways to the
use the IQ Cards will increase. We encourage those who
use the Cards to develop their own applications.
Experiment. Find new ways of creating with the forces
of Light that which you deem desirable, that which is
most appropriate for your growth. Manifest according
to your own inner vision.

Why is it, indeed, that our *intention* to manifest is not always exactly replicated in the actual manifestation itself? Where is the slippage between what we set out to do in consciousness and what eventually results after we have taken action? Sometimes we get precisely what we intend. The reality matches the vision perfectly. On other occasions, the results far exceed the expectations: in our wildest fantasy, we could not have designed a more glorious outcome. Still other situations don't look like anything we had in mind. It's "less than," it's painful, it's drudgery, it's the pits!

If consciousness is indeed cause, how do we become more conscious of consciousness, and thereby more consistently commanding of cause and effect in our lives? I cannot claim to have answered this question for all times and for all people. But I offer here some observations on the matter which might prove instructive:

Generally speaking, the IQ Card forcefields tend to accelerate, amplify, or in some way accentuate outcomes. That which is misaligned in consciousness may become painfully magnified as it seeks alignment. That which is aligned in consciousness can become irresistibly effusive, abundant, and rapturous, challenging our capacity to receive. No matter which way we move on this pain/abundance continuum, the forcefields will push our familiar boundaries and disturb our comfort zones.

There are times, for example, when you may focus your intent in one area but manifest something in another area of your life, quite different from what you intended. Your focus on money might bring vastly increased revenues for your bank account. Or, conversely, it could bring great clarity, pleasant or painful, about whatever is that illusive blockage in your consciousness that persistently limits your abundance. Your focus on a relationship may bring to your awareness that aspect of your consciousness which obstructs your sincere communication from the heart. Your focus on spiritual growth could invoke the presence of angels, or it could return your own judgments right back to you, amplified as an uncomfortable mirror placed before you for your own particular learning.

On another occasion, you might expect the IQ Cards to catalyze a personal creative breakthrough, but instead you encounter your hidden tendency towards limited self-perception. In this instance you could move in and out of feelings of inadequacy, alternating with and counterbalanced by a deep, undeniable knowing of the magnificent radiance of your true being. You may find yourself growing and evolving according to rhythms and tempos that you don't understand. That's perfectly all right. Flow with it. You may extend your mind to comprehend totality, only to discover that you have merely embraced a slightly larger fragment of the whole. Thus, be advised to interpret your results with careful discernment.

What follows are twelve generic applications for the IQ Cards. These suggested uses are offered as general guidelines and have grown out of my workshop, counseling, and research experience. They expand upon the preceding Seven Aspects. Whether you follow the applications given here or create your own, be open to whatever results your actions may bring in their wake, regardless if they are what you expected or not. Learn from and love that which ensues. Keep an open mind and an open heart as you interpret your results. And above all else, keep listening!

Application #1
Empowering Aligned Intent

Commentary

In Proverbs 23:7, King Solomon points to the vital importance of one's inner intent when he states, "As a man thinketh in his heart so is he." Intention sets the tone of consciousness. Whether or not we ever manifest all that we intend, our inner atmosphere, our consciousness, for better or worse, is conditioned by our intentions. That which we desire and intend creates within us particular predispositions, and, according to their nature, these internal subconscious/supraconscious tendencies attract and create our reality.

Intent that is aligned with your own true intuitive knowing (or "Full Potential Self," as identified by Dr. V. Vernon Woolf[1]) attracts situations characterized by love, joy, health, abundance, and understanding. Intent that is *misaligned* with your own true intuitive knowing or "Full Potential Self" results in pain, confusion constriction, frustration, and worse. Moreover, on occasions, aligned intent will challenge your old, dysfunctional ego-realities. If you feel yourself in internal turmoil because your new, clear, heartfelt intent conflicts with your past ego practices, just know that

[1] *Holodynamics,* Dr. V. Vernon Woolf, 1990.

you are probably undergoing a period of spiritual healing.

All of the IQ cards are designed to selectively empower *aligned intent* and *only* aligned intent. The forcefields generated by the geometric patterns have the effect of adding impetus and refinement to individual or group intentions which are in alignment with the innermost truth of the individual or group.

Procedure

1. Write down and focus upon your intentions regarding whatever current situation is of importance to you. How do you feel about them? Do you have any misgivings about your intentions? Can you act with love, compassion, and a clear conscience in attempting to manifest your intentions?

2. Continue to refine your statement of intention until you feel loving, non-judgmental, and at peace with that which you intend.

3. Select your IQ Geometric as outlined under Aspect #2, "Seek Divine Indifference." With your refined statement of intent placed in front of you, focus on your chosen IQ Card. First, focus on the geometric side for three to five minutes. Then turn the card over to the verse and focus on it for a few minutes. Finally, at your own pace, alternate your focus between both sides of the IQ Card. Make notes of all your impressions.

4. Repeat this procedure until you feel clear, loving and empowered with your intent. Then act on it.

Application #2
Uncovering Core Issues

Commentary

We humans engage in various kinds of dysfunctional life dramas, most of which have very little to do with what is really going on deep down inside us: denial, acting out, judging ourselves and others, reacting, rationalizing, self-aggrandizing, self-effacing, unwillingness to give and receive love, controlling behavior, scapegoating, and acting out of ignorance, fear, and anger. The list of emotional histrionics and behavioral disharmonies goes on, with nuances and shadings of intensity ranging from one person to another and from one stage of one's life to another.

Too often hidden from view, there is an awareness of the truly wonderful Light beings that we are — each of us a crystal prism, refracting the Light of our own core being-ness according to our particular pattern of consciousness. If we were to consider the events and the dramas of our life as but symptoms, indicators, or messages about our deeper inner reality, we would indeed be well served.

A core issue is defined here as any aspect of consciousness — a belief, a fear, an action, a memory, a perception, an intention — which is attracting into your life a significant growth opportunity, whether that opportunity takes the form of joy and rapture, or pain and discomfort.

When all about you seems foggy, muddled, and generally askew, use the IQ Cards — cut through to clarity on core issues.

Procedure

1. Set your intention as follows: "to uncover [my] most important current core issue."

2. Define what that core issue is, as you see it.

3. Refer to the Seven Aspects of Intuitive Decision-Making, Chapter Six, and work through each Aspect in sequence from 1 through 7.

Application #3
Creative Brainstorming

Commentary

There are times when you may have the seed thought for a creative project of some kind. It could be a business venture, dance choreography, a musical composition, architectural design, a social function, a book ... whatever. The IQ Cards can be used as a catalyst for creativity, for stimulating and nurturing creative ideas. The procedure below will help you expand your seed thought into a whole plan. During creative brainstorming, it is important to remain open and fluid with your ideas. Do not limit or criticize yourself or others while in the brainstorming mode — just capture ideas. For a brief period allow yourself to feel the freedom of divergent thinking. There will be a time for convergence and drawing conclusions later on.

It is often desirable to work with a partner when brainstorming. This gives you someone to exchange ideas with, and who can also act as scribe, to take down what you are experiencing. Ideally, your partner would also be one who is committed to intuitive listening. Sharing insights with a partner gives more grounding and tangibility to intuitive sense-perception. Such a favorable pairing of minds greatly enhances the intuitive experience.

Procedure

1. Focus on your seed thought. Write it down. Summon as much of your seed thought as you can in the moment and hold it clearly in your conscious mind.

2. Select an IQ Card as per the instructions under Aspect #2.

3. Place the selected card within an arm's length away and gaze steadily at the geometric pattern. Observe, listen, and feel. Hold your focus for about five minutes.

4. Write notes, speak into a tape recorder, or report to your scribe all that you experienced while focusing on the pattern.

5. Next, reflect on the verse of your chosen IQ card.

6. Now integrate your seed thoughts and your new insights into a whole picture, plan, or concept that feels good and seems feasible.

7. Act accordingly.

Application #4
Setting the Environmental Field

Commentary

All spaces have their own unique vibratory character, or unseen "presence," which is conditioned by the forces of nature and by the vibratory quality of human events occurring in a given space. For example, the difference in feeling between St. Paul's Cathedral and Alcatraz prison, even if both spaces were totally vacant, would be obvious to most of us. It is as though some part of the surrounding environment retains a lingering memory, a subtle recording of the events it has witnessed. Our consciousness is capable of detecting such environmental recordings and playing them back to us in the form of feelings, impressions, visual images, sounds, or physical sensations. Just how one receives or registers these subtle environmental stimuli will depend upon one's particular mode of intuitive sensitivity and the degree of its refinement.

With the IQ Cards, you have the option of establishing an environmental forcefield of your own choosing, one which is most conducive to the activities you intend to conduct in a particular space. Regardless of the pre-existing conditions in an office, home, or other space, you can use the cards to create your own forcefield.

If, for example, you work in a busy office with various distractions that hamper your ability to concentrate on your work, card #D-5, "Gaia Growth," generates a forcefield which will help many people keep grounded and focused on the task at hand.

Generally speaking, the following guidelines should suffice to help you select an appropriate IQ Card for setting your environmental field. But beyond the guidelines given here, design your own "etheric environment." Select one, two, three, or four Cards that feel appropriate for you, and energize your own space, according to your needs.

Procedure

1. Get clear on your intention. What is your purpose? What is it you want to achieve or accomplish in the particular environment in which you find yourself?

2. Select an appropriate card(s), as outlined under Aspect #2.

3. Place the card(s) in the chosen environment. Position the card(s) vertically so that the geometric side has no obstructions in front of it. Now operate within the environment as you would normally do. Pay particular attention to any changes or shifts in the way your thoughts and activities flow when the IQ Card(s) is/are in place.

4. Make notes on how you experience yourself and your activities within the forcefield created by the IQ Card(s).

5. Remove the card(s) when you have completed your work in that particular environment.

Application #5
Intuition Self-Training

Commentary

There are those who advocate a holographic cosmology of the universe and its myriad components. In the holographic model, the individual consciousness of each human being is a hologram, a small clone of a vast macrocosm. In a hologram, the totality is fully contained in the smallest part, much like all the genetic information required to clone a person is contained within each cell of an individual's body. An illustration of this holographic hypothesis of the universe is found in a crystal hologram; when broken into smaller pieces, each fractured piece of the crystal contains a complete image of the original object or visual information.

If we adhere to this holographic view of reality, it follows that through the medium of individual human consciousness, we have access to the whole of universal consciousness: the consciousness of the cosmos contained within the consciousness of humankind. Thus all that we seek to know we already have within us.

Analogous to the holographic idea is another approach to understanding our inherent intuitive knowing. It is found in the word "education." The original Latin root word *educo* or *educare* carries the meaning "to bring up" or "to bring out that which is within," to reveal the knowing which one already carries inside. It is with this view that the Socratic method of teaching — named after Socrates and popularized by his student Plato — focuses on revealing one's innate understanding of profound Universal Truths. This is the discipline of intuitive intelligence or *applied intuition* at its best: listening to the vastness of our own inner wisdom.

Procedure

1. Select IQ Card #L5, "Knowing Through Feeling" and place it with the geometric side facing towards you, about twelve to eighteen inches away from yourself.

2. Focus your attention on the center of the geometric and become aware of any physical sensations which you might feel. What other impressions do you get? Hold this position for three to five minutes.

3. Repeat the above two steps on a regular basis, two or three times daily, until you become consciously aware of your various subtle feeling and/ or physical signals that occur with this exercise.

4. Next, after mastering step (3), select Card #D10, "Fertile Expansion," and repeat steps (1), (2), and (3), above. Make notes on any impressions you might receive, and act upon those impressions at your own discretion. Such action steps will often point towards some activity which further enhances your intuitive perception.

5. Finally, after you feel comfortable with your results from step (4), select IQ Card #L8, "The Acumen of Self Counsel," and again repeat steps (1), (2), and (3), above.

6. Become aware of the deeper intuitive self-insight that comes through the use of this particular IQ Card. Pay attention not only to your inner knowing — the subtle energy shifts which occur within — but also be attuned to changes in your tangible world: relationships, circumstances, and your physical body. Your visible, three-dimensional environment will, in some way, mirror back to you the evolving state of your intuitive sense-perception.

Application #6
The Word

Commentary

" ... *the worlds were framed by the word of God ... things which are seen were not made of things which do appear." Hebrews 11:3*

Words are carriers of energy. Aside from whatever information, meaning, or description may be associated with a group of words, they are vessels of force, capable of impacting our mind, emotions, and cell structure in various ways. The words "I love you," spoken gently and sincerely, affect our psycho-biological systems quite differently from the words "I hate you," delivered in harsh, bitter tones.

The verse of the IQ Card has an integral relationship with the geometric pattern on its opposite side; the former is the voice of the latter. Whereas the forcefield of the IQ geometric bypasses language and intellect in reaching into consciousness, the card's verse uses the linearity of language to appeal to the mind. In the terminology of quantum dynamics, the geometric pattern is "wave" and the verse is "particle." Or, bioenergetically speaking, the geometric pattern communicates via the right brain and the verse via the left brain. Both geometric and verse work in tandem towards the same end: to refine the intuitive sense-perception of the individual.

There are various ways in which focus on the verse can assist your knowing. The whole or part of the text may speak directly and clearly to your current situation or to your current issue. Other times there will be a single word or a phrase that jumps out at you and speaks volumes. Often just the title of the card itself will trigger an important insight.

The verse can also generate understanding that is obtained from "between the lines." Reading the verse will sometimes produce feelings, strong or subtle. Listen to these signals. What is the knowing that comes with those feelings?

Procedure

1. Read aloud the verse of your selected IQ Card. Do this several times, being aware of the thoughts and feelings that you experience.

2. Allow your mind to embrace the verse and your issue, or current situation, together as a single unit of energy. Visualize your issue and the IQ Card's verse placed together inside an equilateral triangle:

What happens? In what way does the verse impact your issue? How does your issue/situation appear when you look at it through the filter of your selected verse?

3. Make notes on all impressions catalyzed by reading the verse, as you may later choose to formulate an action plan based upon your insight.

4. Focus on your ability to hear intuitively. After having worked with the IQ Card verse over a period of time, perhaps several days, do you notice any shift in your ability to receive intuitive information, as though a voice were speaking inside your head? Or do words spoken by others trigger some additional knowing for you that goes beyond what they are saying?

5. Maintain modesty. Avoid arrogance. Your growing intuitive prowess is not a weapon to be wielded against adversaries. Rather, it is a service to the Light within yourself and within each person with whom you interact. Speak your words with discernment and sensitivity. Communicate your intuitive information skillfully, with caring and wisdom — always.

Application #7
Invocation

Commentary

In terms of subtle energy dynamics, invocation can be said to occur when your consciousness establishes and holds a thoughtform or thought-pattern of a given frequency or quality. For example, if you or your group hold your focus on The Buddha, you will draw to yourself the energies of love, compassion, and wisdom. Through the principle of resonance, your consciousness attracts to itself — from worlds seen and unseen — complementary feelings, thoughts, and experiences. In other words, "like attracts like," or "what you focus on expands." Choose whatever axiom appeals, but remember that the principle of resonance —*consciousness as cause, attracting complementary vibrations unto itself* — remains valid throughout the worlds of spirit and matter.

Invocation may be intentional — as in a religious or ceremonial ritual— or unwitting, as in long-standing or strongly held beliefs, attitudes, and actions. Either way, the invocation "invokes" or "calls" experiences of like nature back to the originating individual.

In the instance of religious/ceremonial invocation, the collective incantations of the priest and the congregation raise or tune the consciousness of the group to the desired frequency, so that resonance occurs between themselves and the Holy Spirit. And depending on where a given group — sacred or secular — chooses to focus its collective attention, what gets invoked will be more or less holy, or "whole-sum." Fractured, distorted invocations proceed from consciousness that is clouded and divided against itself, while truly holy invocations are the product of clear, loving intention.

The energies of the IQ Cards represent stabilized, harmonious thoughtforms. They establish a resonant interaction between human consciousness and *universal intelligence*. These forcefields can be used to enhance any invocation — religious, traditional, ritual, or personal — providing that the intent of the invocation is to align with the Light of Universal Intelligence in some way.

Procedure

1. Declare the intent of your invocation.

2. Select one or several IQ Cards which feel most appropriate for your particular invocation (refer to Aspect #2, Chapter 6).

3. Place the cards strategically on your desk, your altar, or other appropriate location.

4. Position yourself to experience the optimal effect of the cards — perhaps in the middle of a circular formation, or directly in front of the cards.

5. Proceed with your invocation as you would normally, without any other change.

6. Document your experience. Make notes of what occurs.

Application #8
Thoughtforms and Holodynes

Commentary

While contemporary science tells us that the universe began with a massive explosion of energy/matter (the "Big Bang"), for millennia sages have contended that our world is a creation of God's thought and that "mind stuff" is the primary substance from which all material things arise. Perhaps these two ideas are not mutually exclusive, but such cosmological reconciliation is the topic of other volumes. For our purposes in using the IQ Cards, we need only accept the concept that "thoughts are things," with unique forms, patterns, and frequencies. Moreover, it is important to note that there are natural laws which govern the behavior of thought energies. For example, thought energies are governed by the principles of resonance. They group and congregate based upon shared or similar frequencies of vibration, i.e. "like thoughts attract like thoughts." In this way, individual thoughts congregate and thoughtforms of varying quality are created.

Dr. V. Vernon Woolf[2] uses the term "holodyne" to define thoughtforms. He writes:

"[Holodynes] are the fundamental unit of the holodynamic universe; the first order of organization on the manifest plane; a multidimensional holographic unit of memory storage. Holodynes are thoughtforms with causal potency, which behave like tiny entities within the mind, creating,

[2] Woolf, *op. Cit.*, p. 214

directing, shaping and influencing its thought streams ... holodynes are responsible for ego-states, engrams, frames of thought, inner dialogues, personality characteristics and behavior patterns. They are formed from sensory input, modeling, experience, imprinting, genetic inheritance, imagination, and parallel worlds."

The forcefields of the IQ Cards operate in, and directly upon, the plane of thoughtforms or holodynes. It is the hypotheses of this writer that the following minimal effects apply with respect to IQ Card forcefields and thoughtforms:

A. The forcefield of each geometric pattern constitutes a thoughtform itself. These IQ forcefields are what Dr. Woolf defines as "mature" or "updraft holodynes," which influence the flow of the mind towards order, vitality, love, peacefulness, union, and intuitive knowing. By contrast, "immature" or "downdraft holodynes" influence the flow of the mind towards disorder, dis-ease, fear, denial, judging, anger, and ignorance of truth.

B. When an IQ Card is properly selected and its forcefield interfaced with one's own personal thoughtforms, the card creates an atmosphere which supports an appropriate and harmonious updrafting or maturation of one's own holodynes or thoughtforms.

C. There is a causal potency with each IQ card. The subtle causal forces associated with each card are capable of catalyzing and shifting the energies of consciousness towards specific updraft patterns of growth, expansion, and intuitive perception.

D. The IQ Card forcefield operates as a primary holodyne on the holodynamic plane and as such, conditions or modifies the energy of the *quantum wave*. According to Dr. Woolf, "The quantum wave is a universal field containing all possibilities on the unmanifest plane for any circumstance … it is composed of an infinite number of 'quanta' or 'bits and pieces' … From the intuitive perspective, it is a field in which all possibilities exist without distinction until a mind focuses upon the field with specific intent."[3]

Therefore, the Card's forcefield supports and parallels the function of one's Full Potential Self, and very likely exerts some form of aligning and information-encoding influence upon cellular DNA.

Procedure

At this time, there is no particular procedure for this application. This commentary is offered as background information and as a catalyst for those who might be interested in pursuing the subject further.

Application #9
Bioenergetic Research

Commentary

For millennia, various wisdom teachings have held that our human anatomy comprises certain invisible

[3] Woolf, *op. Cit.*, p. 217

light frequencies and subtle energies. Ancient texts teach us that these pre-physical subtle bodies constitute a causal, formative matrix without which the physical body could not exist. Now through the investigations of such researchers as Dr. H. S. Burr (a neurophysiologist of Yale Medical School), Dr. Rupert Sheldrake (a British microbiologist), and Dr. Gaston Nassens (a French-Canadian orthobiologist), modern science is beginning to discover what the Rishis[4] knew over 3,000 years ago. Burr and Sheldrake describe the function of subtle energy fields which are fundamental to our physical existence, while Nassens, through his unique microscope design, has identified subcellular light particles in the body, which he calls "somatids." With modern science and ancient wisdom beginning to converge through the courageous work of some contemporary pioneers, we may expect further breakthrough discoveries.

Additionally, we know that our invisible energy fields constitute a bridge between our mind/emotions and our physical organism. Patterns in consciousness impact our cells via our subtle bodies. The work of neurosurgeon Dr. Norman Shealy and intuitive diagnostician Caroline Myss, as well as Louise Hay and others, speak to the issue of patterns in consciousness affecting one's state of health. Informal preliminary investigations with the IQ Cards suggest that the forcefields generated by the cards' geometric patterns are probably capable of impacting and altering the human subtle bodies. Early testing via bio-kinesiology showed marked shifts in releasing long-standing, debilitating, mental/emotional blockages in the

[4] masters of wisdom, exalted teachers of the early civilizations

consciousness of test subjects. Further testing of the IQ Cards with various subtle-energy monitoring techniques is recommended and encouraged.

Procedure

There is no particular procedure for this application, at this time. The above information is offered here as background and catalyst for those researchers who might be interested in pursuing further investigations.

Application #10
Clarifying Priorities

Commentary

Are there times when you seem to be out of touch with what your core issues really are? Perhaps you feel unable to grasp or articulate what is really going on. Or maybe you would simply like to set a positive tone, identify your theme for the day, before starting out in the morning. Use the IQ Cards to identify your true priorities. This is a situation where you seek orientation: to know consciously how your own inner wisdom perceives what is of primary importance in your life right now. Such a focus allows you to move through your day — indeed through your life — following a path of least resistance. Just imagine the economy of time, resources, and emotional energy you would achieve if you only acted upon that which your inner guidance points out as relevant! Living each day according to your true priorities, you will accomplish more, feel more fulfilled, and probably have a lot more fun.

Procedure

1. Let your intention be to identify that which is your most relevant current priority.

2. Take a few deep breaths and relax. Place yourself in a meditative, contemplative, receptive frame of mind. This sets your personal environment for an Intuitive-Mind-Directed Selection of the appropriate IQ Card.

3. Select an IQ Card. Read the verse. What is its message to you? Make notes.

4. Focus on the Card's geometric pattern three to four minutes. What impressions, if any, do you receive?

5. Review any insights gained from this exercise and proceed with your life, guided by this inner knowing.

8

*"Intuition is soul guidance ... Every man has the power of
intuition, as he has the power of thought. As thought can
be cultivated, so intuition can be developed. In intuition we
are in tune with Reality — with the inner laws governing
the spiritual world ... It is through intuition that humanity
reaches Divinity ... intuition is what all the great savants
and prophets of the world possessed."*

Paramahansa Yogananda
Founder, Self-Realization Fellowship

CELEBRATING DIVERSITY, RECOGNIZING ONENESS

Primal Identity

Perhaps the single most dominant challenge of our
contemporary world society — our global village comprised of individuals, ethnic groups, and nations — is
our need to truly understand ourselves and each other.
It is hoped that this volume, together with the
accompanying IQ Cards, will help advance such
understanding.

A person is far more than meets the cursory glance
of the eye, the rational scrutiny of the intellect, or the
ethnic judgments of society. The primary point of one's
identity, the supreme and enduring reality of each
human being, is that of a loving, individualized Spirit
— clothed first in light and then in flesh.

Before gender and physical anatomy, before race,
ethnicity, or culture, before religion, political affiliation,

or profession — even before our family of origin and the circumstances of our birth and rearing — we are unified light-units of Spirit evolving our respective consciousnesses along discrete paths, according to the guidance of Universal Intelligence. This primal reality of who we are precedes and commands all else. However exalted or debased, the popular images of our Earth life (career, relationships, possessions, etc.) are but transitory ego-vehicles, whose function is to serve our primal reality as Spirit evolving in awareness.

Therefore, if we would categorize people in order to identify them here in our Earth society, let it be according to how effectively they manifest their true identity as loving light-units. Social labels and stereotypes based upon such temporal aspects as skin color and ethnicity merely enslave our higher sense-perceptions to the tyranny of "illusions posing as reality." Your closest of kin may or may not be a blood relative, or one attired in the same skin color as your own, speaking in your tongue, and practicing your particular religious rituals.

You will know your siblings of the Soul, not by their incarnate outfits or by definitions provided by social prejudice, but by the intense affinity, the resonance of Spirit which registers clearly in your heart. Recognize as your kindred — whatever their color or circumstance — those who choose to align with the Light of their own inner spirit, for in doing so they necessarily align with the Light within us all. Herein lies true brotherhood.

There can be no harmony between races, genders, or nations without The Intelligence of The Heart —

that aspect of each person's consciousness that knows innately the true identity of self and others. The course of peace consists in making this inner wisdom conscious practice. History, intellect, science, money, politics, and diplomacy are inadequate vehicles for healing the wounds that rend the matrix of light connecting our human family. Gnosis, direct intuitive knowing, speaking and listening from the heart, must accompany all our decision-making, all our attempts to build bridges of understanding between peoples.

Wherever we, as humankind, truly seek understanding and harmony in preference to conflict and warfare, such solutions are available within our willingness to bring The Intelligence of The Heart to bear upon our issues — both personal and worldly. Ultimately, the celebration of diversity is a celebration of spiritual (not necessarily religious) oneness. This is an acknowledgment of the dance of a singular Universal Light, operating through the infinite hues which constitute the variety of the human experience — a cosmic lesson from which we may all learn and grow — uniquely, yet together.

Here are some general considerations and guidelines for using the IQ Cards as a means of promoting inter-ethnic harmony:

Willingness

Parties must first be willing to *celebrate*, rather than resist, fear, or agonize over their cultural/ethnic differences. By whatever means one manages to arrive at this important first step in the process, *the will to inter-*

ethnic harmony is essential for success in celebrating cultural diversity. Willingness sets the field, for just as the "will to live" is fundamental to a fulfilling life, so too is the "will to harmonize" crucial in bringing about real harmony between culturally diverse peoples. There needs to be an ongoing commitment from all parties, individuals, and groups: to act from the heart in seeking the highest possible degree of alignment; to stay the course; to not quit; to not give up or give in; to achieve harmony by collectively celebrating our uniqueness.

Healing The Past

Unexpressed, pent-up feelings — emotional toxicity held over from times past — can sabotage well-intended intercultural cooperation. At the other extreme, incessant bickering, blaming, and non-forgiveness is equally counter-productive and leads nowhere. Before a group can move to substantive issues, they may first need to clear the air. Wherever such a need for group emotional catharsis exists, seek competent professional help in moving through this phase of the group process in a skillful, timely manner. Release pain and forgive as a means of preparing the way for true harmony. While protracted venting of emotions is counter-productive, removing old obstacles to trust is essential. Once sufficient emotional clearing has occurred in order to permit a genuine group focus on the real issues, follow the guidelines set out in Chapter Six under the Seven Aspects of Intuitive Decision-Making.

Intention

Innate wisdom tells us that whatever we envision, wherever we focus our consciousness as *cause*, there too will our *effect* be. Witness the fact that over the centuries, man's focused intention to fly has resulted in his mastery of the skies with sophisticated vehicles of flight. Let us, then, collectively set our intention to resolve inter-ethnic conflict and move up to the celebration of cultural diversity. If our true intention is to produce "win-win" solutions for all peoples, then that is exactly the result we will achieve.

Of Rainbows and Orchestras

How can there be a true understanding of the part, without some comprehension of the whole of which the part is an integral constituent?

An array of color stretches across the sky and we recognize it as something we call a rainbow. We may choose to focus on that part of the light spectrum which we know as "blue," but how far can our understanding of reality go, if "blue" is not understood within its relationship to red, yellow, green, and violet — the totality of the light spectrum? Whatever differences exist between the races of humankind — genetic distinctions, natural talents, feeling tendencies, and so on — they are there by cosmic design. Each racial/ethnic group brings something magnificent to add to the whole, like the eighty-eight keys of a piano, or the various instruments that comprise an orchestra. If the drum were not truly a drum, or the violin not truly a violin, then the finished product, the harmony, rhythm, power, grace ... the balanced and blended moods of the composition could not come into being.

It is timely now that we, as humankind, reflect upon the import of our daily doings, our centuries of cynicism, of forcing our egoistic wills upon one another. We would do well to contemplate the will of Universal Intelligence, for it permeates and impacts the progression of all things — solar systems, cellular biology, and the affairs of human beings. It is this greater Cosmic Will — still palpable through the din of our most cherished illusions — that guides each of us towards our true destiny: acquiring the consciousness of a Full Spectrum Human Being.

The "Full Spectrum Human Being" is one who comprehends the richness of racial and ethnic diversity, rather than fearing the differences; one who ranges across the whole continuum of perception, from the subtleties of the Spirit to the mechanics of the mind; one who designs with the wisdom and the tenderness of the heart, and then implements that design with the sharpness and efficiency of the intellect. As faithful companions on your journey through this Earth-life, and towards Full Spectrumship, I offer you the following couplets as procedure for this final application. Engage them under any circumstance, whenever you feel the inclination, and acknowledge the energy that rises from within your own consciousness in response:

I INVOKE THE PRESENCE OF MY ETERNAL BEING,
THAT LIGHT OF LOVE THAT AIDS MY SEEING.

MY INTENTIONS ARE FOCUSED AS MY WISDOM LEADS,
MY ACTIONS FROM MY SOUL PROCEED.

GLOSSARY

Balanced Perception   Using intuition and intellect in harmonious tandem. Balanced perception recognizes that both rational and intuitive sources of information are important in order to function effectively in the world. See *Intelligence of The Heart.*

Cause and Effect   Over 3000 years ago, the ancient Hermetic wisdom teachings set forth the law of cause and effect, which states that everything happens according to law and that nothing ever merely happens. This principle holds that "chance is but a name for law not recognized; there are many planes of causation, but nothing escapes the law."

Consciousness   The totality of that agency through which we have the capacity to be aware of our existence. For ease of understanding, the whole of consciousness can be sub-divided into discrete functional aspects, e.g. five-sense physical awareness, intuitive awareness, intellectual awareness, subconscious awareness, cellular and molecular awareness, and so on.

Devas/Devic   A category of loving, endearing energy-beings, most often associated with the plant and mineral kingdoms of nature. Devas communicate telepathically with those humans who are capable of seeing or feeling their presence. Devas are frequently described as fairies and elves.

Direct Cognition   Awareness of reality, and of truth, through intuitive perception, without the intervention of intellectual or rational modes of thought. See *Intuition* and *Gnosis*.

Etheric Environment   A defined space, such as a room or a section of a room, which has been energized by a configuration of one or more IQ Geometrics. *Etheric environment* is the author's term for identifying a subtle-energy frequency shift that occurs when the IQ Geometrics are used to impact one's immediate surroundings.

Human Energy Field   Subtle light frequences emitted by the dynamics of the human body-mind-spirit, and invisible to normal sight. Sometimes referred to as the aura, various aspects of the multi-dimensional human energy field have been described by both ancient mystics and contemporary research scientists. The findings of Dr. Harold S. Burr, Dr. Robert O. Becker, and Dr. Rupert Sheldrake are among the works of notable modern-day investigators.

Intellect   That aspect of consciousness by which we comprehend and communicate via linear processes such as logic, language, and rational thought.

[The] Intelligence of The Heart   A term believed to have originated in the wisdom schools of ancient Egypt. *The Intelligence of the Heart* refers to balanced knowing that embraces both intuition and intellect. While such knowing may at times be instantaneous, it is always characterized by clarity and accuracy of perception, and by the absence of conflict between the heart and the head.

Intuition   That aspect of consciousness by which we comprehend and communicate via non-linear processes such as direct perception, feelings, and inner knowing.

Intuitive Intelligence   A term coined by the author, *intuitive intelligence* refers to the knowing, the gathering, and the processing of information, via one or more of our faculties of inner knowing. Such faculties may include clairvoyance or various other forms of intuition and direct perception. Intuitive Intelligence identifies a natural and innate information-sorting feature of our consciousness that is not restricted by the rules of rational, trained, or artificial intelligence.

Intuitive Sense-perception   The innate human faculty for detecting the presence of subtle energies that do not register upon our normal five senses. See *Intuition*.

Geometric/Geometric Forcefields   The IQ card geometric drawings in this volume, which are designed to create subtle patterns of pre-physical energies. The IQ Geometrics work on the basis of intersecting angles which create a "standing wave" frequency, detectable by extended sense-perception. The Pythagorean school and other wisdom-school traditions used different variations of the geometric principles for expanding the capacity of human consciousness. Investigators from Plato to Buckminster Fuller have recognized the vital role that geometry can play in enhancing the quality of human consciousness.

Gnosis   Knowledge of spiritual truth; knowing gained through direct perception. The real Gnosis is transcendent: insight that goes beyond the appearances which many people accept as the only reality. There

were religious groups called Gnostics who were promi-
nent in Alexandria, Palestine, Syria, and neighboring
areas, just prior to and including the period of Jesus. A
fundamental tenet of Gnostic belief is that of self-
knowledge: the idea that by understanding the Light
within one's own consciousness, one comes to the true
knowledge of God.

Holodynes   In his book, *Holodynamics,* Dr. V.
Vernon Woolf defines holodynes as follows: "Holodynes
are thought-forms with causal potency which behave
like living entities within the mind, creating, directing, shaping, and influencing its thought-streams.
Holodynes are responsible for ego-states, frames of
thought, inner dialogues, personality characteristics,
and behavior patterns."

Homeopathy   The science of homeopathy was
developed by the German physician, Dr. Samuel
Hahnemann, during the early 1800s. Homeopathy rests
upon the "law of similars," or "like cures like." If, for
example, one is suffering from symptoms similar to
those produced by poisoning by snake venom, homeopathy might actually prescribe a very highly diluted
dosage of snake venom as a remedy. The natural base
substances for making homeopathic remedies are
drawn from the animal, vegetable, and mineral kingdoms. Homeopathic remedies tend to be deep-acting
— even effecting the subtle bodies — in reaching the
cause of illness. Eliminating harmful toxins from the
body is a fundamental feature of how homeopathics
work in their healing action.

Mirroring   The phenomenon of experiencing
something of your own consciousness reflected back

to you in the behavior and attitudes of others. Often the person with which you are dealing, or the situation in which you find yourself, "holds up a mirror to you" — for better or worse — that you might gain further insight and self-knowledge.

Multiple Channels   See *Multi-Sensory Input*.

Multi-Sensory Input   When extended beyond "normal" range, each of our five senses — hearing, sight, touch, taste, and smell — becomes "extrasensory." Such extended sense-perception can be called intuitive and is capable of bringing us information about the subtle realities of our surrounding environment which escape ordinary perception.

Principle of Resonance   This is the concept of "like attracts like." For example, the idea that similar mind energies and similar thought patterns have a natural attraction for each other is based on resonance. Resonance — whether of minds or of molecules — explains the spontaneous affinity that frequently occurs between two or more independent systems.

Psionic   Psionic is used here to define a broad spectrum of subtle-energy applications which combine the energies of consciousness with the technology of electronics. Various instruments and devices are used to help detect, amplify, or otherwise manipulate subtle-energies. Dowsing, divination, radionics, radiesthesia, and certain aspects of energy medicine are some of the areas of "mind-machine circuitry" which can be classified under the heading of psionics.

Quantum Dynamics   The new physics; a scientific theory applicable to all aspects of the created universe: everything from subatomic particles, to biological systems, to celestial galaxies. The theory of quantum dynamics holds that all phenomena are ultimately comprised of vibrating fields and energy waves — quanta — which demonstrate the properties of both particle and wave.

Radiesthesia   That discipline of subtle-energy research and practice which employs specialized pendulums, and related devices, as adjuncts to intuitive sense-perception. When intuitive techniques were suppressed during the Dark Ages in Europe, the practice of radiesthesia was kept alive by an underground which included Catholic priests. During the early 1900s, two French priests, Abbé Bouly and Abbé Mermet, were distinguished for their roles in advancing the technology of radiesthesia in the modern world. Abbé Bouly is credited with coining the term radiesthesia, meaning "the sensing of subtle radiations." Radiesthesia has applications in medicine, geology, and archeology, as well as many other areas of investigation.

Rational mind See *Intellect.*

Sensory Response   Automatic nerve responses triggered by the forcefields of the IQ Geometrics. Some individuals may notice a spontaneous neurological response when exposed to the IQ Geometrics, such as a slight muscle twitch or a deeper, slower breathing pattern. This is the innate intelligence of the body signalling its sensitivity to the presence of the energies created by the geometric.

Soul-Self   That aspect of the individual's consciousness that is eternal, all-knowing, and all-loving. Soul-Self refers to that aspect of one's being that is both the repository for, and the director of, all earthly experience gained via the personality-self and the physical-self.

Still, Small Voice See *Intuition*, *[The] Intelligence of The Heart*, and *Intuitive Intelligence*.

REFERENCES

Jose and Miriam Arguelles, *Mandala*, Boulder, CO: Shambhala Publications, 1972.

Victor R. Beasley, *Your Electro-Vibratory Body*, Boulder Creek, CA: University of the Trees Press, 1979.

Victor R. Beasley, *Subtle-Body Healing*, Boulder Creek, CA: University of the Trees Press, 1979.

Marta and Walter Burleigh, *The Balancing Program*, Tucson, AZ.

Manley P. Hall, *The Secret Teachings of All Ages*, Los Angeles, CA: The Philosophical Research Society, 1977.

Willis Harman, *Global Mind Change*, Sausalito, CA: Institute of Noetic Sciences, 1988.

The Holy Bible.

Murry Hope, *The Way of Cartouche*, New York, NY: St. Martin's Press, 1985.

William Kingsland, *The Gnosis and Christianity,* Wheaton, IL: The Theosophical Publishing House, 1975.

Stanley Krippner/Daniel Rubin, *The Energies of Consciousness*, New York, NY: Interface, 1975.

The Law of Order, Atami, Japan: Church of World Messianity, 1966.

Michael Ray and Rochelle Meyers, *Creativity in Business*, New York, NY: Doubleday, 1989.

Three Initiates, *The Kybalion*, Chicago, IL: The Yogi Publication Society, 1940.

Lao Tsu, *Tao Te Ching*, Translated by Gia-Fu Feng and Jane English, New York, NY: Vintage Books, 1972.

Aubrey T. Westlake, *The Pattern of Health*, Berkeley, CA & London, England: Shambhala, 1974.

V. Vernon Woolf, *Holodynamics*, Tucson, AZ: Harbinger House, 1990.

Paramhansa Yogananda, *Autobiography of a Yogi*, Los Angeles, CA: Self-Realization Fellowship, 1981.

APPENDIX

Reader's Support and Dialogue

Feedback To The Author

Dr. Beasley welcomes your feedback on *Intuition by Design*. All observations and suggestions are appreciated. We encourage your reports on results achieved from using the IQ Cards. Also, please indicate whether we have your permission to quote from your report in our future publications.

Speaker Services

Some of the Oughten House authors and staff are available for speaking engagements, workshops, and organizational and interpersonal consulting. We have programs on intuition, communications, and self-empowerment. We also offer expertise in publishing (editing, production, marketing, and distribution), ascension information, and networking. Should your organization be interested in hosting an Oughten House representative, please write stating the nature of your request. We will provide you with further information.

Resources

The publisher has listings of professionals in such areas as Applied Intuition, Health and Wellness,

Spiritual Counseling, and other services, in some parts of the United States and the world. Whenever possible, Oughten House will match your needs for professional services with those who provide such services. If you are in need of the professional services of someone who is compatible with the principles, the concepts, and the values expressed in this book or other Oughten House publications, please let us know. State the kind of service you require and include your name, address, telephone number, and fax number (if any).

The decision to use the services of any professional on our list is completely your own. Screen each one carefully to assure that he/she meets with your personal standards. Oughten House seeks only to provide our readers with quality options. We do not assume responsibility for your choices.

Service-Providers

If you are a professional service-provider who feels compatible with the principles, concepts, and values expressed in this book (or other Oughten House publications), let us know. If you would like to be included in our referral list, please provide the following information:

✧   Name, address, telephone number, and fax number (if any).

✧   Description of service(s) provided.

✧   A brief personal biography and summary of your professional experience.

✧ A listing of all degrees, certificates, qualifications, and recognition relevant to the services you provide, including dates and the institutions or sources from which they were received.

✧ A brief statement of your purpose in choosing to be included on the Oughten House listing of professional service-providers.

✧ A sample brochure and/or literature which details your services, fees, and availability.

Networking

If you are interested in either forming or joining a support group or discussion group, centered around this book or other Oughten House publications, please let us know. We will refer you to others in your area with similar interests. Also, if you expect to move to a new city or to another country, we may be able to refer you to individuals or groups in your new location.

ABOUT THE AUTHOR

Dr. Beasley is an Intuitive Intelligence Consultant, helping people reach new levels of creative expression in their personal and professional lives. He guides individuals and groups in listening to themselves, so that they come to consciously recognize the creative solutions which they already carry within.

His academic background includes an undergraduate degree in anthropology and a doctorate in psychology, with postgraduate investigations in Europe and Asia.

Dr. Beasley's experience in the fields of consciousness research and awareness training covers more than eighteen years. His two previous books, *Your Electro-Vibratory Body* and *Subtle Body Healing,* focus on the use of intuitive techniques as applied to Energy Medicine.

Under the auspices of the US State Department, Dr. Beasley represented the United States in Latin America and the West Indies in the areas of social development, cultural exchange, and race relations.

As an associate of *Resource Systems*, a Los Angeles based consulting firm, Dr. Beasley conducts corporate training programs in Intuitive Decision-Making and Teambuilding.

Victor and his wife, Michelle, reside in Phoenix, Arizona, where he does personal counseling, training, and consulting.

About the Publisher and Logo ...

The name "Oughten" was revealed to the publisher fourteen years ago, after three weeks of meditation and contemplation. The combined effect of the letters carries a vibratory signature, signifying humanity's ascension on a planetary level.

The logo represents a new world rising from its former condition. The planet ascends from the darker to the lighter. Our experience of a dark and mysterious universe becomes transmuted by our planet's rising consciousness — glorious and spiritual. The grace of God transmutes the dross of the past into gold, as we leave all behind and ascend into the millennium.

Publisher's Comment ...

Our mission and purpose is to publish ascension books and complementary material for all peoples and all children worldwide.

We currently serve over twenty authors who have books, manuscripts, and numerous tapes in production. Our authors channel Sananda (Jesus), Ashtar, Archangel Michael, St. Germain, Archangel Ariel, Hilarion, Mother Mary, Kwan Yin, and other Ascended Masters. We are in the process of extending this information to all nations, through foreign translations. Oughten House Publications welcomes your support and association in this momentous and timely endeavor. We urge you to share this information with your friends and families, and to join our growing network of like-minded people. A reply card is included for your convenience. Blessings and peace be with you always.

Oughten House Publications

Our imprint includes books in a variety of fields and disciplines which emphasize the rising planetary consciousness. Literature which relates to the ascension process is our primary line. We are also cultivating a line of thoughtful and beautifully illustrated children's books, which deal with spirituality, angels, mystical realms, and God, the Creator. Our third line of books deals with societal matters, personal growth, poetry, and publications on extraterrestrials.

The list that follows is only a sample of our current offerings. To obtain a complete catalog, contact us at the address shown at the back of this book.

Ascension Books & Books for the Rising Planetary Consciousness

The Crystal Stair: A Guide to the Ascension, by Eric Klein. — ISBN 1-880666-06-5, $12.95

An Ascension Handbook A practical, in-depth, how-to manual on the ascension process, by Tony Stubbs.
— ISBN 1-880666-08-1, $11.95

Bridge Into Light: Your Connection to Spiritual Guidance A how-to book on meditating and channeling, by Pam and Fred Cameron. (A companion tape is also available.) — ISBN 1-880666-07-3, $11.95

The Inner Door: *Channeled Discourses from the Ascended Masters on Self-Mastery and Ascension*, by Eric Klein.

Volume One: ISBN 1-880666-03-0, $14.50
Volume Two: ISBN 1-880666-16-2, $14.50

What Is Lightbody? Offers a twelve-level model for the ascension process, leading to the attainment of our Light Body. Recommended in *An Ascension Handbook*, this book gives many invocations, procedures, and potions to assist us on our journey home. Related tapes available. By Tashira Tachi-ren — ISBN 1-880666-25-1, $11.95

Lady From Atlantis Millenium after millenium, male rulers have repeatedly failed to bring peace to this planet. Now Ascended Lady Master Shar Dae returns to modern America, to pursue her goal of world peace and the ending of duality. By Robert V. Gerard — ISBN 1-880666-21-9, $11.95

Transformational Tools

We offer an ever-expanding selection of transformational tools to assist you in your journey back to mastery. These include books and tapes, with such titles as *The Thymus Chakra Handbook*, *Reality Maintenance 101*, *On Eagle's Wings*, *E.T. 101*, and a series of tapes by Tashira Tachi-ren. For information on these and other titles in this category, please call or write for our free catalog.

Discourses & Channeled Material

Hear the voices and experience the energies of our authors, on companion tapes to *Bridge Into Light* and *The Extraterrestrial Vision*. In addition, we offer many tapes on other spiritual and metaphysical subjects, such as *Parallel Realities*, *Birthing the Era of God*, *The Feminine Aspect of God*, and *Preparation for Ascension*. They are listed and described in our free catalog. Write or call for your copy now!

Children's Books and Tapes

Books and tapes in this category include titles such as *Nature Walk*, *Mary's Lullaby*, *Song of Gothar*, and *Bear Essentials of Love*. Although primarily intended for children and adults who interact with children, they speak to the "child" within us all. For a full list of titles in this category, please call or write for our free catalog.

Music Tapes

We carry many titles of spiritually-based music, including both vocal and instrumental types. They collectively comprise a cornucopia of moods and sounds. Create your own "ascension chamber" whenever you play them — at home or wherever your journey takes you. For a listing of available titles, call or write for our free catalog. A reply card is bound into this book for your convenience, or you may reach us at the location listed on page 127.

Other Ascension Tools and Materials

We distribute many other items to assist you on your spiritual path. They include Ascension Cards and titles such as *The Extraterrestrial Vision*, *An Act of Faith*, *The P'taah Tapes*, *Earth's Birth Changes: St. Germain through Azena*, and many more. Ask for our free catalog; we stand ready to serve you!

Reader Networking and Mailing List

The ascension process presents itself as a new opportunity and reality for many of us on Planet Earth. Oughten House Publications now stands in the midst of many Starseeds and Lightworkers who seek to know more. Thousands of people worldwide are reaching out to find others of like mind and to network with them.

You have the opportunity to stay informed and be on our networking mailing list. Send us the enclosed Information Reply Card or a letter. We will do our best to keep you and your network of friends up to date with ascension-related literature, materials, author tours, workshops, and channelings.

If you have a network database or small mailing list you would like to share, please send it along.

Catalog Requests and Book Orders

Catalogs will gladly be sent upon request. Book orders must be prepaid: check, money order, international coupon, VISA, MasterCard, and Discover Card accepted. Include shipping and handling (US postal book rate): $3.50 first book; add 50¢ for each additional book. Send orders to:

OUGHTEN HOUSE PUBLICATIONS
P.O. Box 2008
Livermore • California • 94551-2008 • USA
Phone (510) 447-2332
Fax (510) 447-2376

ATTENTION: BUSINESSES AND SCHOOLS!

OUGHTEN HOUSE books are available at quantity discounts with bulk purchases for educational, business, or sales promotional use. For details, please contact the publisher at the above address.

IQBD 2-1

From:

_____

_____

_____

"Ascension Books for the Rising Planetary Consciousness"

OUGHTEN HOUSE PUBLICATIONS
P.O. Box 2008
Livermore, CA 94551-2008
USA